CONTENT

Section 1

2

Section 2

30

Section 3

50

58

SECTION 1

ACROSS

1) Calculate 17 – 10 – 5
2) What is the sum of 25, 5 and 3 ?
3) _ _ + 10 = 88
4) What is the next even number after 68 ?
5) What is the product of 25 and 2 ?
6) Calculate 5^2 plus 10
8) Subtract 11 from 6^2
9) What is the difference between 20 and 4 ?
13) What is the next odd number after 73 ?
18) Divide the product of 5 and 10 by two ?
19) What is eight more than 20 ?
22) What is the sum of 10, 8 and 4 ?

DOWN

7) What is the next prime number after 3 ?
10) Which one of these numbers is not a prime number: 5, 7, 8, 11, 13 ?
11) 25 - 10 - _ = 10
12) What is eight lots of 11 ?
14) What is two more than 2^3 ?
15) Divide 18 by three
16) What is the difference between 41 and 38 ?
17) What is the next highest prime number after 7 ?
20) Calculate 107 - 99
21) Calculate $7^2 - 10 - 3^2$
23) What is the total of eleven, four and 6 ?

SUM MEANS TO ADD

The HINTS are there to help you...read them through from time to time.

HINTS

+ Addition, Add, Sum, Plus, Increase, Total

– Subtraction, Subtract, Minus, Less, Difference, Take Away, Deduct

× Multiplication, Multiply, Product, By, Times, Lots of

÷ Division, Divide, Goes Into, How Many Times

A prime number can only have two factors, which is 1 and itself.

All prime numbers are greater than 1

When a number multiplies by itself, it gives a square number,
e.g. 6^2 means 6 squared which is 6 x 6

A cube number is the answer when a number multiplies by itself three times,
e.g. 27 (cube number) = 3 x 3 x 3

NUMBERS

Use the clues to complete the CrossMaths

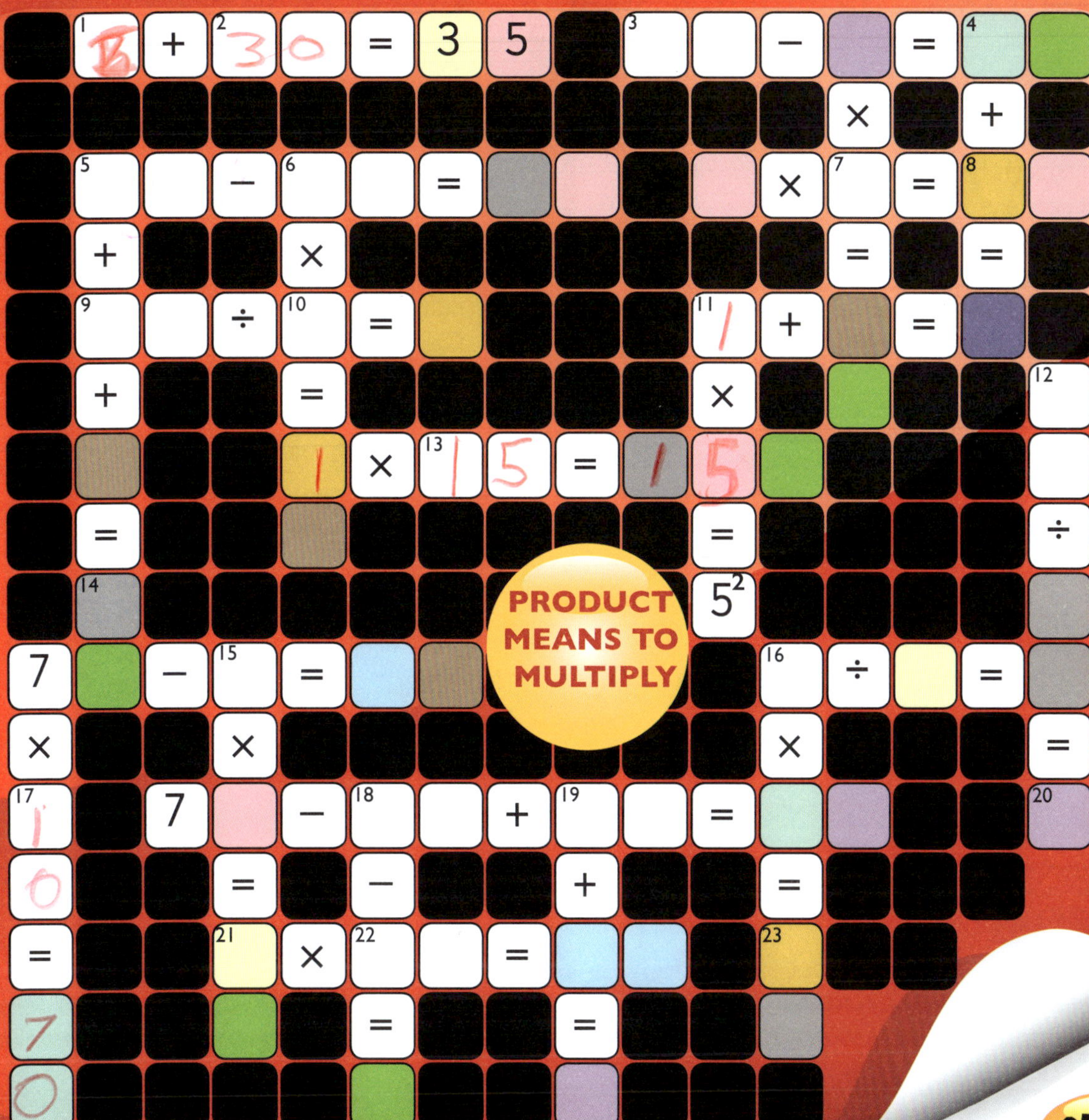

SKIPS™

SKIPS CHALLENGE TIME!

Well Done! Now that you have completed the CrossMaths, it is SKIPS Challenge Time. Copy the numbers from the coloured tiles in the CrossMaths to the matching coloured boxes below to complete the sentences.

Lou Roll has two questions for you.

A) Why was ☐ scared of ☐? Because ☐ ate ☐.

B) Why didn't number ☐ like number ☐?

Because it knew number ☐ was odd.

PLACE VALUE

Use the clues below to complete the CrossMaths

ACROSS

2) Calculate 0.6 + 0.5
4) What is 9.57 rounded to one decimal place ?
5) Calculate 3.2 + 1.4
9) Which digit has the value of units in 236 ?
11) Calculate 2.4 + 0.6 + 4
13) Round 10.6 to the nearest whole number
14) Calculate 0.5 x 10
19) What value does the digit 8 have in 281.53 ?
20) Round 53.7 to the nearest 10
22) Calculate 55 ÷ 10

DOWN

1) What value does the digit 4 have in 146 ?
3) Which digit has the value of tens in 151 ?
6) Which digit has the value of tenths in 3.24 ?
7) Round 33 to the nearest 10
8) Round 4.647 to 2 decimal places
10) Calculate 0.25 x 10
12) What is 4.65 rounded to the nearest whole number ?
15) Calculate 76.13 – 21.13
16) What is 2.54 rounded to 1 decimal place ?
17) Calculate 0.65 + 0.6 + 0.55
18) Which digit has a value of hundredths in 25.376 ?
21) Which digit has a value of tenths in 30.24 ?

HINTS

Every Digit in a Number has a Place Value.

Before a decimal the place values are known as: Thousands (Th), Hundreds (H), Tens (T), Units (U).

The place value after a decimal are Tenths ($\frac{1}{10}$ ths), Hundredths ($\frac{1}{100}$ ths) and Thousandths ($\frac{1}{1000}$ ths).

E.g. Take a look at the number 5412.321 below.

Th	H	T	U	•	$\frac{1}{10}$	$\frac{1}{100}$	$\frac{1}{1000}$
5	4	1	2	•	3	2	1

What Is Rounding?

Rounding means reducing the digits in a number whilst trying to keep its value similar.

Common Rounding Method:

1) Decide which is the last digit to keep.
2) Leave it the same if the next digit is less than '5'.
3) Increase it by '1' if the next digit is '5' or more.

E.g. Round 0.127 to 2 decimal places:

This is the second decimal number

↓

0.127

↑

This is the third decimal number

Solution:

The third decimal number, '7' which is greater than '5', so we add '1' and drop the rest of the decimal numbers:

Answer: 0.13 i.e. 0.127 = 0.13 (2dp)

Remember to use the **HINTS** to help as you work through the CrossMaths.

SKIPS CHALLENGE TIME!

Well Done! Now copy the numbers from the coloured tiles in the CrossMaths to the matching coloured boxes below and answer the following questions.

Jack Pot thinks he has won some money on the lottery. The following numbers make up his possible prize winnings. Can you rearrange the numbers to see:

A) What is the largest amount of money he can win ?

£_ _ _ _ _

B) What is the smallest amount of money he can win ?

£_ _ _ _ _

FACTORS AND MULTIPLES

Use the clues below to complete the CrossMaths

ACROSS

3) What do the factors of 2 add up to ?
4) How many factors does the number 6 have ?
7) Which of these is not a factor of 21:
   1, 2, 3, 7, 21 ?
8) How many factors does the number 19 have ?
15) What do the factors of 15 add up to ?
16) How many factors does the number 9 have ?
17) How many factors does the number 16 have ?
19) What do the factors of 45 add up to ?
20) Which of the following numbers is a multiple of 6 and 7:
    26, 28, 32, 36, 42 ?
21) How many factors does the number 69 have ?

DOWN

1) What do the factors of number 11 add up to ?
2) What is the highest factor of number 20 ?
5) Which one of these is a multiple of 3 and 15:
   10, 20, 25, 30, 35 ?
6) What do the factors of number 7 add up to ?
9) How many factors does the number 10 have ?
10) Which one of these is a multiple of 4 and 11:
    4, 11, 22, 44, 60 ?
11) Which one of these numbers is not a multiple of 2 and 6:
    6, 12, 18, 23, 24, 30 ?
12) How many factors does the number 20 have ?
13) How many factors does the number 40 have ?
14) Which one of these numbers is a multiple of 8 and 12:
    12, 18, 36, 40, 48 ?
18) How many factors does the number 23 have ?

**2 X 3 = 6
6 IS THE MULTIPLE OF 2 AND 3**

HINTS

FACTORS are all the numbers that divide exactly into another number without leaving a remainder. When looking for factors it is best to write them in pairs,
e.g. factors of 20 are:
(1, 20), (2, 10), (4, 5)
You can see from this that the number 20 has 6 factors.

The MULTIPLE is the answer when you multiply factors together, e.g.
4 x 1 = 4
4 x 2 = 8
4 x 3 = 12
That is, 4, 8 and 12 are multiples of 4

All numbers have an even number of factors unless that number is a square number, e.g.
16 is a square number (4 x 4)
The factors are (1, 16), (2, 8), (4, 4)
You can see from this that 16 only has 5 factors.

5 x 5 written in INDEX NOTATION is 5^2

It will help you to memorise the HINTS in the CrossMaths

SKIPS CHALLENGE TIME!

Well Done! Now copy the numbers from the coloured tiles in the CrossMaths to the matching coloured boxes below and answer the following question.

Rufus Leaking **needs to buy some new tiles for his roof.**

If a tile cost £[ ].[ ][ ], how many tiles in total can he buy with £[ ][ ]? = [_ _]

FRACTIONS

Use the clues below to complete the CrossMaths

ACROSS

2) Calculate $\frac{2}{11} + \frac{3}{11}$

4) Three out of four children drink milk. What is this as a fraction ?

5) Which one of these fractions is the same as $\frac{50}{100}$: $\frac{10}{30}$ $\frac{25}{75}$ $\frac{3}{4}$ $\frac{1}{2}$ $\frac{50}{10}$?

6) Reduce $\frac{12}{33}$ to its lowest term

8) Reduce $\frac{12}{22}$ to its lowest term

9) Simplify $\frac{20}{5}$

12) Three out of nine children wear hats. What is this as a fraction in its lowest term ?

13) Calculate $2\frac{1}{2} - \frac{3}{2} - \frac{1}{2}$

18) Which one of these fractions is the same as $\frac{10}{40}$: $\frac{1}{3}$ $\frac{1}{5}$ $\frac{1}{2}$ $\frac{1}{4}$ $\frac{10}{20}$?

21) Calculate $1\frac{1}{2} \div 3$

DOWN

1) Calculate $\frac{1}{4} + \frac{1}{4}$

3) What fraction of this shape is shaded ?

7) What fraction of this shape is not shaded ?

10) A quarter of a number is 2. What is the number ?

11) Four out of 6 children walk to school. What is this as a fraction in its lowest term ?

14) Which one of these improper fractions is the same as $2\frac{1}{2}$: $\frac{7}{2}$ $\frac{3}{2}$ $\frac{5}{2}$ $\frac{10}{6}$ $\frac{9}{3}$?

15) Calculate $\frac{8}{10} + \frac{2}{5} - \frac{4}{10}$ (Write your answer in its lowest term)

16) What is 20 out of 60 as a fraction in its lowest term ?

17) $\frac{75}{100} = \frac{\square}{4}$

19) $\frac{15}{24} = \frac{\square}{8}$

20) What is a third of 12 ?

22) Which one of these improper fractions is the same as $1\frac{1}{2}$: $\frac{9}{3}$ $\frac{14}{10}$ $\frac{9}{2}$ $\frac{3}{2}$?

HINTS

A FRACTION is the number of equal parts in a whole number,
e.g. $\frac{3}{4}$ means 3 equal parts out of 4.

Improper fractions can be changed to mixed numbers when the bottom number divides into the top number to give a whole number and a fraction as a remainder. e.g. $\frac{14}{5} = 2\frac{4}{5}$

The top part of the fraction is called a <u>numerator.</u>
The bottom part of a fraction is called a <u>denominator</u>.
Before you can add or subtract fractions, the fractions need to have a common denominator. Look for the lowest common denominator. (L.C.D). e.g.
$\frac{1}{3} + \frac{2}{5} = \frac{5}{15} + \frac{6}{15} = \frac{5+6}{15} = \frac{11}{15}$

Simplify / Reducing Fractions - Divide the top and bottom by the highest number (Highest Common Factor, H.C.F)that can divide into both numbers exactly until we can't go on anymore. The top and bottom of the fraction must always be a whole number. You can only multiply or divide, never add or subtract, to get an equivalent fraction. e.g. simplify: $\frac{75}{150} = \frac{3}{6} = \frac{1}{2}$

When multiplying fractions we multiply the <u>numerators</u> with each other and multiply the <u>denominators</u> with each other.
e.g. $\frac{1}{2} \times \frac{3}{4} = \frac{1 \times 3}{2 \times 4} = \frac{3}{8}$

To divide fractions one simply inverts the second fraction and then multiply like before.
e.g. $\frac{3}{4} \div \frac{1}{2} = \frac{3}{4} \times \frac{2}{1}$ (inverted) $= \frac{6}{4}$

reduced: $\frac{6}{4} = \frac{3}{2} = 1\frac{1}{2}$

Read through HINTS first, they will help you to understand fractions.

SKIPS CHALLENGE TIME!

Well Done! Now copy the numbers from the coloured tiles in the CrossMaths into the matching coloured boxes below and answer the following questions.

Can you help *Yura Stinker* to simplify these fractions?

A) $\frac{36}{44}$ = $\frac{\square\square}{\square\square}$ = $\frac{\square}{\square}$

B) $\frac{20}{80}$ = $\frac{\square\square}{\square\square}$ = $\frac{\square}{\square}$

DECIMALS

Use the clues below to complete the CrossMaths

ACROSS

2) Calculate 10 x 0.25 x 2
3) What value does the digit 1 have in the number 2415 ?
7) What is the sum of 9.78, 13.65 and 6.57 ?
9) Calculate 1.25 x 4
10) Calculate 0.125 x 4
14) Round 10.776 to 2 decimal places
17) Which one of these numbers is closer in value to 4.5:
4.15, 4.33, 4.75, 4.99 ?
18) Calculate 21.03 minus 4.33
19) Calculate 25.2 divided by 6
20) Calculate 27.6 divided by 3

DOWN

1) Calculate 0.04 x 100
4) Calculate 0.4 x 0.5
5) Write in figures one thousand and ten
6) Calculate 1.25 x 16
8) Calculate 71 x 2 ÷ 100
11) Round 6.117 to 2 decimal places
12) What value does the digit 1 have in the number 3145.26 ?
13) Write in figures nine hundred and ninety seven
15) What is the product of 0.5 and 32 ?
16) Which digit has a value of hundredths in 432.15 ?

HINTS

When we write numbers, the position (or 'place') of each number is important, 'Place Value'.

Decimal Numbers are Whole Numbers plus Tenths, Hundredths, Thousandths, etc.

When adding or subtracting decimals write down the numbers, one under the other, with the decimal points lined up. Put in zeros so the numbers have the same length. Then add or subtract normally, remembering to put the decimal point in the answer.

When multiplying decimals multiply normally, ignoring the decimal points. Then put the decimal point in the answer - it will have as many decimal places as the two original numbers combined.

e.g. 0.04 x 1.1
Multiply without decimal point 4 x 11 = 44
Now 0.04 has 2 decimal places and 1.1 has 1 decimal place.

So the answer has to have 3 decimal places: 0.044

When dividing use long division (ignoring the decimal point). Then put the decimal point in the same spot as the number being divided.
E.g. 9.1 ÷ 7 =

We now have, ignoring the decimal point 7 | 91 (answer 13)
Put the decimal point in the answer directly above the decimal point in the number that has been divided.

7 | 9.1 (answer 1.3) The answer is 1.3

SKIPS™

The HINTS are there to help you to understand measurements...have a look.

SKIPS CHALLENGE TIME!

Well Done! Now copy the numbers from the coloured tiles in the CrossMaths to the matching coloured boxes below and answer the following question.

Ken U. Seemee **made it to the** ***'Invisible Man look a like'*** **finals.**

[ ][ ][ ][ ] tickets were sold for the open air show, but it rained heavily on the night and only [ ][ ][ ][ ] people attended.

How many people with tickets did not attend the show? = _ _ _ _

• DECI

E.g. $\frac{3}{4} = \frac{75}{100} = 0.75$

Step 1) Find a number you can multiply so that the bottom of the fraction will make 10, or 100, or 1000, or any 1 followed by 0's.

Step 2) Multiply both top and bottom by that number.

Step 3) Then write down just the top number, putting the decimal point in the correct place (one space from the right hand side for every zero in the bottom number).

E.g. $0.625 = \frac{0.625}{1} = \frac{625}{1000} = \frac{25}{40} = \frac{5}{8}$

Step 1) Write down the decimal divided by 1

Step 2) Multiply both top and bottom by 10 for every number after the decimal point. (For example: if there are two numbers after the decimal point, use 100, if there are three use 1000, etc. Here we have three numbers after the decimal point so multiply top and bottom by 1000.

Step 3) Simplify (reduce) this fraction.

FRACTIONS

E.g. $\frac{1}{4} = \frac{1}{4} \times \frac{100}{1} = \frac{100}{4} = 25\%$

Step 1) Multiply fraction by $\frac{100}{1}$

Step 2) Multiply across / Reduce

Step 3) Add the % sign

CONVERSION CHA

MALS •

E.g. 9% = $\frac{9}{100}$ = .09 = 0.09

Step 1) 9% means 9 out of 100

Step 2) Divide by 100
(Move decimal point two places to the left).

E.g. 0.14 = 0.14 x 100 = 014. = 14%

Step 1) Multiply by 100 (move decimal point two places to the right)

Step 2) Add percentage sign %

PERCENTAGES

E.g. 7.5% = $\frac{7.5}{100}$ = $\frac{75}{1000}$ = $\frac{3}{40}$

Step 1) Create a fraction by placing the decimal number as the top part and the 100 as the bottom of the fraction.

Step 2) Move decimal point to the end of the number on top part and for every positioned move add a 0 to the number underneath.

Step 3) Simplify /Cancel

RT FOR DECIMALS

FRACTIONS, DECIMALS, PERCENTAGES

Use the clues below to complete the CrossMaths

ACROSS

1) Write 0.3 as a fraction
2) Write 70% as a decimal
3) Which digit has a value of thousandths in 3455.549 ?
4) What is 25% of 16 ?
6) Write $\frac{3}{25}$ as a percentage
12) Write $\frac{9}{20}$ as a percentage
14) Write $2\frac{1}{10}$ as a decimal
15) Write this improper fraction as a decimal: $\frac{6}{5}$
19) What is 10% of 780 ?
20) Write $\frac{9}{50}$ as a decimal

DOWN

5) Write 70% as a fraction in its lowest term
7) What percentage of £200 is £16 ?
8) What is 0.04 as a percentage ?
9) Write 60% as a decimal
10) Write $4\frac{1}{5}$ as a decimal
11) What percentage of 25 is 5 ?
13) What is 1% of 200 ?
16) What is 0.08 as a percentage ?
17) Write $\frac{2}{20}$ as a decimal
18) What is 12 out of 150 as a percentage ?

0.25 as a percentage = 0.25 x 100 = 25%

HINTS

Decimals, Fractions & Percentages are different ways of showing the same value.

e.g. $\frac{1}{2} = 0.5 = 50\%$

A percentage is the top part of a fraction when its bottom number is 100.

e.g. $\frac{1}{2} = \frac{50}{100} = 50\%$

Use the CONVERSION CHART on pages 12-13. It will show you how to convert between decimal, fractions and percentages.

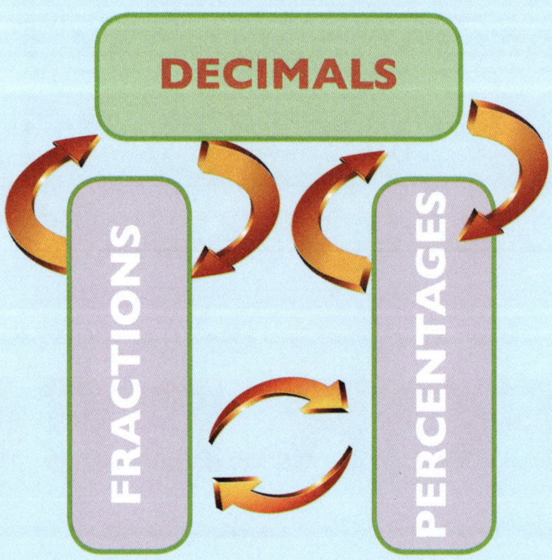

Don't forget to check the HINTS!

SKIPS CHALLENGE TIME!

Well Done! Now copy the numbers from the coloured tiles in the CrossMaths to the matching coloured boxes below and answer the following question.

This season the '*Night-Mares*' horse riding team have been bad. They have lost [green][yellow] % of their [purple][grey] trials.

How many trials have they won? = _ _

Perimeters, Areas, Compound Shapes

Use the clues below to complete the CrossMaths

ACROSS

2) What is the missing width for this rectangle, which has an area of 32 mm^2?

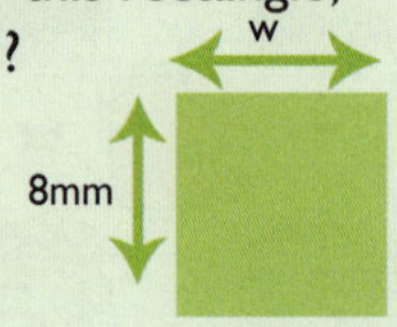

3) What is the area of the triangle?

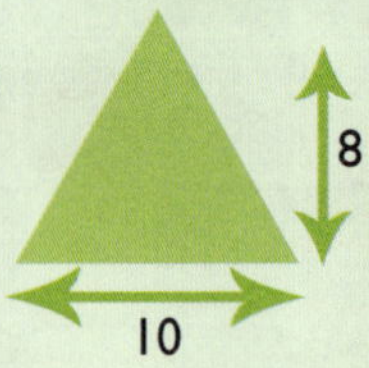

6) What is the area of a triangle that has a height of 8 cm and a base length of 8 cm?

7) What is the area of a triangle that has a base length of 14 m and a height of 4 m?

From the compound shape shown answer the following:

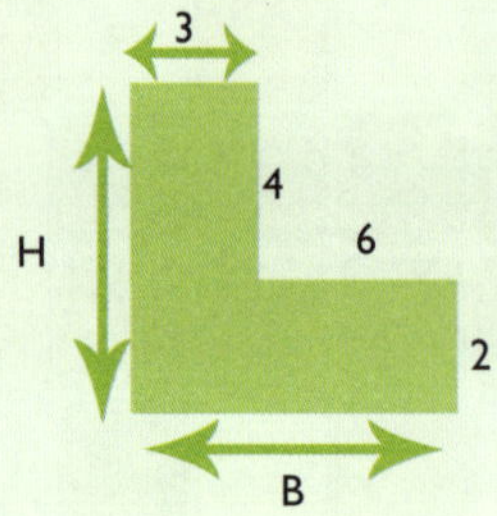

8) What is the height H ?

9) Base B length

10) Perimeter of compound shape

From the following shape what is:

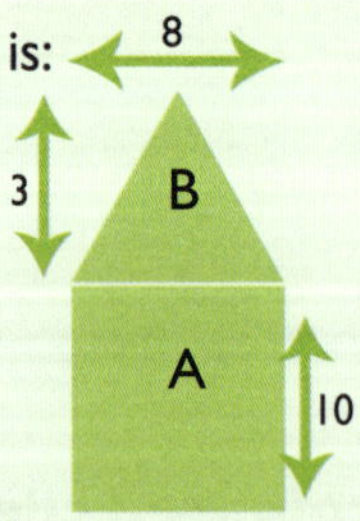

17) Area of A

18) Area of B

19) Total area

Area is how much space a shape is covering

DOWN

1) What is the area of the square?

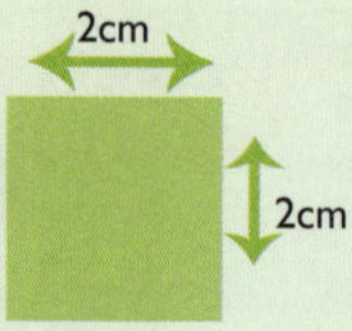

4) What is the length of a square that has an area of 64 cm^2?

5) What is the perimeter of a rectangle that is 9 m by 3 m?

11) What is the area of a triangle that is 16 cm by 3.5 cm?

12) What is the perimeter of a square that has a side length of 11cm?

From the following shape what is:

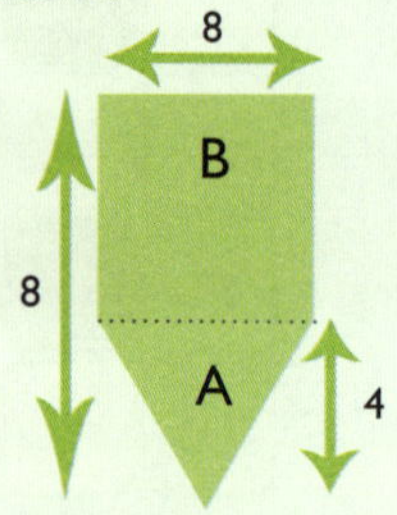

13) Area of A

14) Area of B

15) Total area of shape

16) What is the area of a rectangle that has a perimeter of 24 cm and a length side of 4 cm?

20) What is the height of a triangle that has a base length of 6 cm and an area of 30 cm?

Area of triangle = $\frac{1}{2}$ b x h

The perimeter is the addition of the outside lengths of the shape

Area of a square or rectangle = L x W

SKIPS™

Are you ready for the SKIPS Challenge?

SKIPS CHALLENGE TIME!

Well Done! Now copy the numbers from the coloured tiles in the CrossMaths to the matching coloured boxes below and answer the following questions.

A) What is the area of the triangle?

= ___ ___ ___ m²

[brown][blue] m

[pink][yellow] m

B) The perimeter of a rectangle is [lilac][brown] cm

The length of a rectangle is [pink][brown] cm

1) What is the width of the rectangle?

= ___ cm

2) What is the area of the rectangle?

= ___ ___ cm²

ANGLES

Use the clues below to complete the CrossMaths

ACROSS

What are the missing angles:

1) X

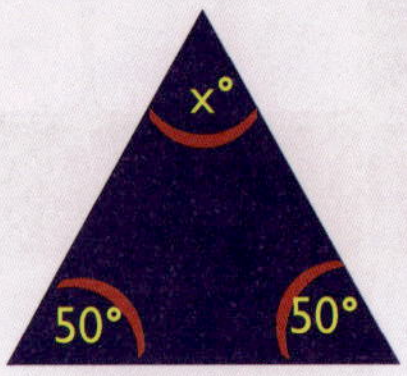

2) X

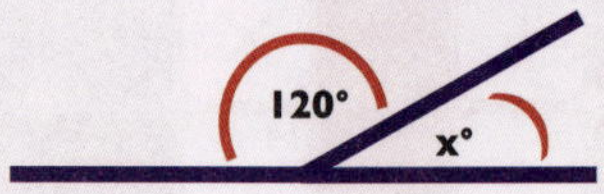

The pie chart shows how lazy Sacha spends his day (24 hours). How long does he spend doing the following:

8) Sleeping (S) hrs.

9) Activities (A) hrs.

10) Lessons (L) hrs.

11) Playing (P) hrs.

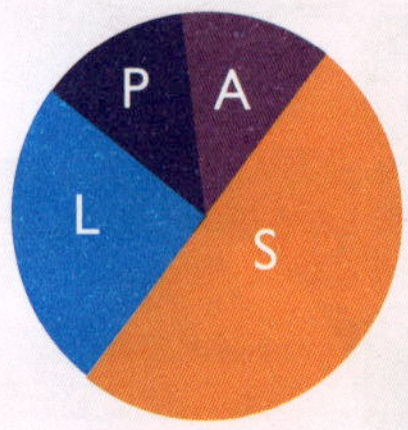

What are the missing angles in the following diagrams:

12) X

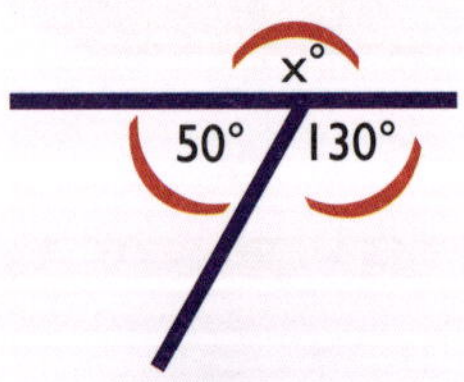

16) X

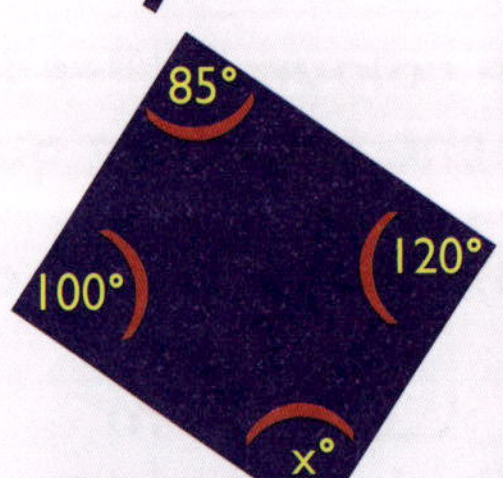

18) X

19) Y

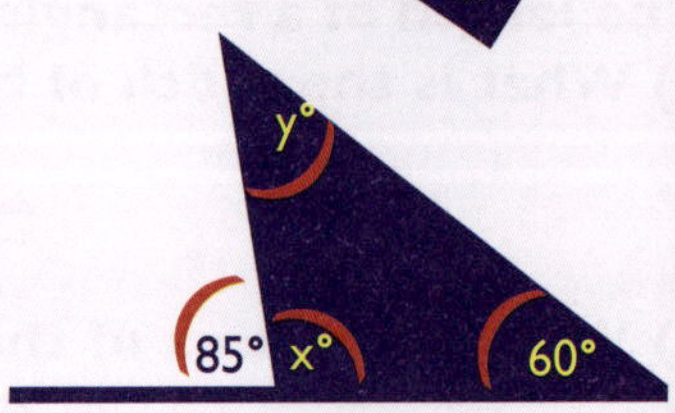

DOWN

Work out the missing angles of these triangles.

	1st angle	2nd angle	3rd angle
3)	55	50	?
4)	40	?	95
5)	?	60	40
6)	69	?	42

What are the missing angles of the shapes below:

7) X

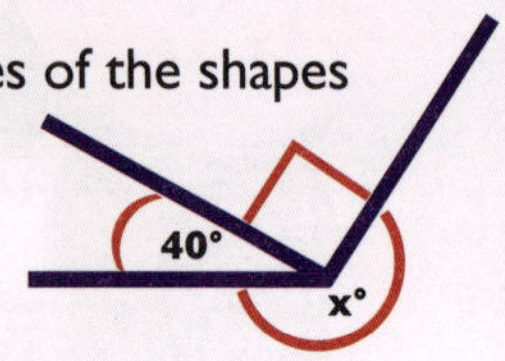

12) X

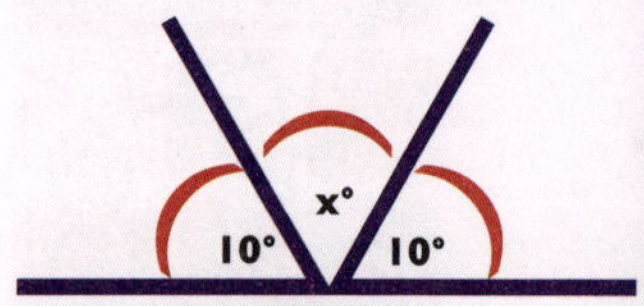

13) X

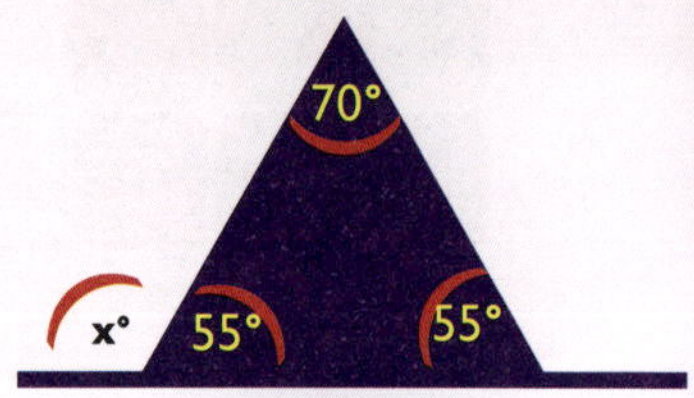

14) X

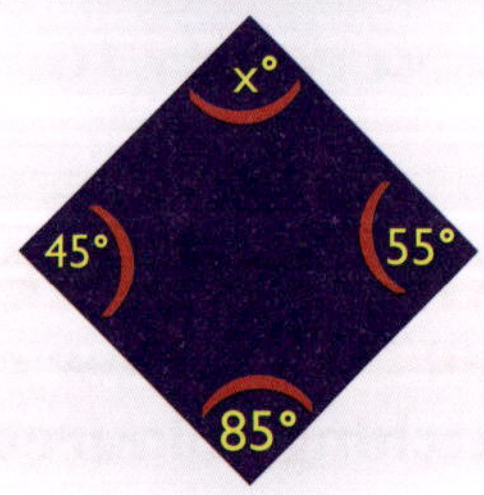

15) X

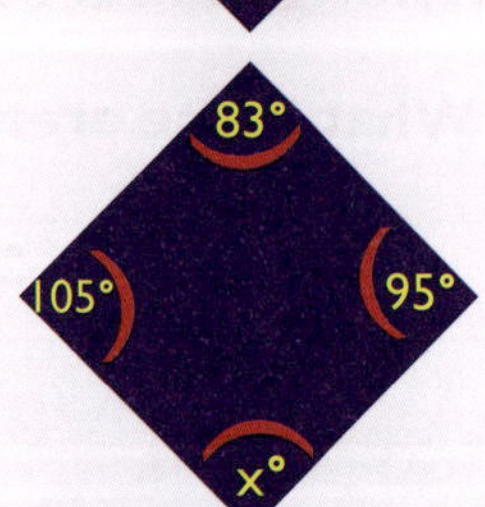

17) X

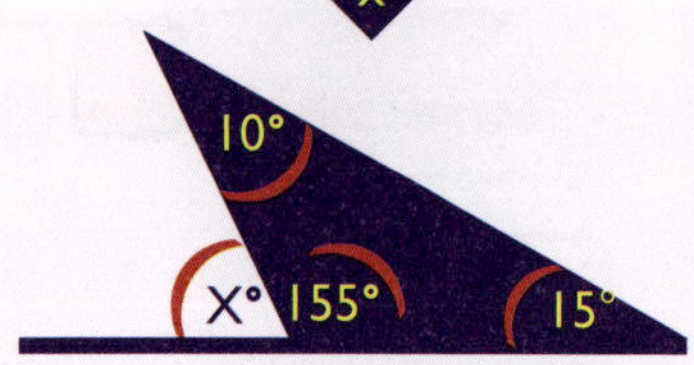

SKIPS™

SKIPS CHALLENGE TIME!

Well Done! Now copy the numbers from the coloured tiles in the CrossMaths to the matching coloured boxes below and complete the sentences.

Can you help *Barry Schmelly* with his angles and fill in the missing numbers for him?

Acute angles are less than ☐☐°

Right angles are ☐☐° exactly

Obtuse angles are greater than ☐☐° but less than ☐☐☐°

Reflex angles are greater than ☐☐☐°

Fantastic

MEASUREMENTS

Use the clues below to complete the CrossMaths

ACROSS

1) How many millimetres in 4 centimetres ?

2) How many centimetres are there in 20 millimetres ?

6) How many grams are there is 6 kilograms ?

10) How many centimetres are in half a metre ?

12) What is my speed if it takes me 7 hours to travel 49 km ?

13) How far in kilometres will I go if I travel for 4 hours at 4 km/h ?

14) Convert 6.392 kg into grams

16) In how many hours from 19.00 will it be midnight ?

19) If a car travels at an average speed of 40 km/h for 15 hours, what distance does it cover ?

20) How many cm are there in 3.03 m ?

DOWN

3) How many millimetres are there in 97 cm ?

4) How many minutes are there in ten hours ?

5) Dan Singh arrives at the concert at 17.40. The concert starts at 6 o'clock. How many minutes does he have to wait ?

7) Convert 0.103 L to ml

8) How many metres are there in 0.32 km ?

9) How many minutes are there in one hour and ten minutes ?

11) In the long distance Rodney jumps 197 cm and Cassandra jumps 2.18 m. What is the difference in length between their jumps measured in cm ?

15) How many hours are there in 240 minutes ?

17) Joy rides her bike and travels 45 km in 5 hours. At what speed was she travelling ?

18) Robbie Rayne starts a telephone conversation on his mobile phone at 13.03 and ends it at quarter past two that afternoon. How many minutes did his conversation last ?

HINTS

To convert from one unit to another you have to use the following:

mm → cm (÷ 10) cm → m (÷ 100) m → km (÷ 1000)

mm ← cm (x10) cm ← m (x100) m ← km (x1000)

g → kg (÷ 1000) ml → L (÷ 1000)

g ← kg (x 1000) ml ← L (x 1000)

$\text{Speed} = \frac{\text{Distance}}{\text{Time}}$ i.e. $S = \frac{D}{T}$

Therefore $D = S \times T$ and $T = \frac{D}{S}$

(Remember algebra and the balancing method)

Always change minutes into hours when given a question. This is done by dividing the minutes by 60

e.g. 20 mins = $\frac{20}{60}$ = $\frac{1}{3}$ hrs

The HINTS are there to help you to understand measurements...have a look.

SKIPS CHALLENGE TIME!

Well Done! Now copy the numbers from the coloured tiles in the CrossMaths to the matching coloured boxes below and answer the following question.

Dennis Racket buys □ . □ kg of oranges. He gives □/□ of them to his friend *Jim Shorts*.

How many grams of oranges does *Dennis* have left? = ___ ___ ___ g

BRACKETS

Use the clues below to complete the CrossMaths

ACROSS

1) $2 \times (6+6)$
2) $(8+9+15) \div 2$
3) $(27 \div 3) \times (28 \div 4)$
5) $(69 \div 3) \times (55 \div 11)$
7) $(38 + 17 + 65) - (16 + 11 + 18)$
8) $(2.45 + 8.7 + 3.85) \times (2 \div 0.5)$
12) $(\frac{1}{8} + \frac{3}{8} + \frac{1}{2}) \times (\frac{1}{2} + \frac{1}{4} + \frac{1}{4})$
16) $(33.03 + 5.84 + 11.13) \times (4 \times 2.5)$
17) $(38.8 + 26.6 + 44.6) - (19 \times 4) + 16$
21) $(31 + 80 - 47) \div (4\frac{1}{3} + 3\frac{2}{3})$
24) $(5^2 - 10) \times (10^2 \div 10)$

DOWN

4) $(450 + 350) - (125 - 50)$
6) $(80 - 45 + 31) - (80 \div 5)$
9) $(1.23 - 0.66 + 0.43) \times (1.25 \div 5)$
10) In Harry's Happy Shopper shop a pencil cost 50p and pens cost 75p each. How much will it cost to buy 7 pencils and 2 pens ? (Answer in pounds)
11) $(23 \times 0.5) \div 10$
13) $(22.2 \times 10) - (27.5 + 69.5 + 100)$
14) $(3.5 \times 4) \times (4\frac{1}{4} + \frac{3}{4})$
15) $(225 \div 25) \times (60 \div 30)$
18) $(0.5 \times 0.5) + (\frac{1}{2} \times \frac{1}{2})$ Write your answer as a decimal.
19) $(3\frac{1}{2} + \frac{3}{4} + 3\frac{1}{4}) \times (3.25 + 6.75)$
20) $(4 \times 11 \div 2) \times (25 \div 5 \times 3)$
22) In Harry's Happy Shopper shop a chocolate bar cost 65p and chewing gum cost 25p. How much will it cost to buy 5 chocolate bars and 3 packets of chewing gum ? (Answer in pounds)
23) $(8^2 - 4^2) \div (2^2 + 2^3)$

HINTS

Always do the calculation in the brackets first.

Turn everything inside a bracket into a single number, then continue with rest of the equation.

Brackets are great to group information when problem solving, e.g.

If pens cost 20p each and pencils cost 15p each, how much would 4 pens and 3 pencils cost in total?

Here we can use brackets to group the information.

Cost of 4 pens = (4 x 20)

Cost of 3 pencils = (3 x 15)

Total cost = (4 x 20) + (3 x 15)

= 80p + 45p

Total = £1.25

Brackets are used to group information

Have you remembered to check the hints...they will help you.

SKIPS CHALLENGE TIME!

Well Done! Now copy the numbers from the coloured tiles in the CrossMaths to the matching coloured boxes below and answer the following question.

Bill Ding wishes to buy litres of paint. How much cheaper is it to buy $2\frac{1}{2}$ - litre tins than one litre tins?

= £ __ . __ __

£ .

£ .

ALGEBRA

Use the clues below to complete the CrossMaths

ACROSS

1) If x + 12 = 15, what is x ?

2) If 5y = 20, what is y ?

8) 10^2 → [-8^2] → [+ 4] → x

9) If 100 ÷ y = 10, what is y ?

11) If x = 6, what is x^2 ?

16) The sum of three numbers is 16. The other two numbers are 4 and 5. What is the value of the third number ?

17) Rishi bought some sweets for 65p and a packet of crisps for 66p. How much change did he get from £1.50 ?

18) If 2(x + 4) = 4x – 2, what is the value of x ?

19) x → [multiply by the sum of 3 and 7] → 50

20) 12.5 → [multiply by the product of 2 and 5] → x

DOWN

3) If 25 – x = 20, what is x ?

4) If 15 – x = 11, what is x ?

5) 25 → [x 2] → [÷ 10] → [+ 3] → x

6) 3 → [add nine] → [multiply by two] → x

7) x → [multiply by itself] → 16

10) If 2(x + 4) = 28, what is x ?

12) If 5a + 9 = 6a – 3, what is a ?

13) If x = 3, what is x^3 ?

14) If x = 6, what is the value of 3x – 10 ?

15) Sacha receives 20p change from £2.00 after buying 6 cartons of orange juice. Find the cost of each carton of orange juice ?

HINTS

In algebra the letters represent numbers and can be written as the following e.g.

a + a + a = 3a
a x a = a^2 (not 2a)
c x c x c = c^3 (not 3c)
a x b x 4 = 4ab (put numbers first then letters in alphabetical order)
x ÷ y = $\frac{x}{y}$ (a division is usually written as a fraction)
3(a + b) = (3 x a) + (3 x b) = 3a + 3b

Re arranging a formula is known as the balancing method. This means whatever you do to one side of the equation, you must do exactly the same to the other side.

Function Machines have 3 parts

IN → [FUNCTION] → OUT

IN - A number that goes into the machine
OUT - A number that comes out of the machine
FUNCTION - The calculation that the machine does.

There are some extra **HINTS** in the CrossMaths to help you!

SKIPS CHALLENGE TIME!

Well Done! Now copy the numbers from the coloured tiles in the CrossMaths to the matching coloured boxes below and answer the following questions.

Mr Lu Zer **loves algebra. Can you help him calculate the following function machines?**

A) [mint green box] → add to the sum of [brown box] and [red box] → = __ __

B) [gold box] → add to the product of [grey box] and [dark purple box] → = __ __

Fun, isn't it?

AVERAGES

Use the clues below to complete the CrossMaths

ACROSS

1) What is the mean of this set of numbers:
4, 6, 8, 6 ?

2) What is the mode of this set of numbers:
7, 9, 11, 9, 7, 6, 9 ?

7) Find the mode of this set of numbers:
5, 4, 7, 4, 5, 6, 5

13) The mean age of four girls is 9. If the ages of three girls 7, 9 and 8, what is the age of the remaining girl ?

Sheikh Yiboudi goes to dance lessons on three separate days. The length of the classes were 44, 40 and 44 minutes.

14) What was the mode ?

15) What was the median ?

16) What is the range of this set of numbers:
925, 980, 1010, 900, 1080 ?

17) The mean of four numbers is 10. Three of the numbers are 10, 13 and 9. Find the value of the fourth number ?

19) What is the range of this set of numbers:
305, 342, 256, 200, 210 ?

20) What is the mean of this set of numbers:
25, 45, 20 ?

DOWN

3) What is the mode of this set of numbers:
101, 100, 101, 103, 100, 103, 100 ?

4) What is the range of this set of numbers:
3, 2, 4, 3, 6, 5 ?

5) What is the mean of this set of numbers:
11, 7, 13, 7, 14, 8 ?

6) If the total of four numbers is 32, what is the mean ?

8) The mean of 5 numbers is 20. Four of the other numbers are 20, 26, 14 and 32. What is the value of the missing number ?

9) What is the median of this set of numbers:
10, 14, 9, 15 7, 11, 4 ?

10) What is the range of this set of numbers:
55, 50 68, 92 90 ?

11) The average of four numbers is 40. Three of the numbers are 32, 44 and 46. What is the value of the missing number ?

12) The range of four numbers is 40. The lowest number is 8 and two of the other numbers are 25 and 34, what is the fourth number ?

18) What is the range of this set of numbers:
132, 88, 142, 100, 90 ?

RANGE: The difference between highest and lowest number

SKIPS CHALLENGE TIME!

Well Done! Now copy the numbers from the coloured tiles in the CrossMaths to the matching coloured boxes below and answer the following questions.

Can you help *Ollie Day* to find the following:

A) What is the mode? = __ __

B) What is the mean? = __ __

C) What is the range? = __ __

Ratios and Handling Data

Use the clues below to complete the CrossMaths

ACROSS

2) Simplify the ratio to its simplest form. Find the value of y.
40 : 12 = y : 3

4) The ratio of oranges to apples in a basket is 3 : 5. If there are 9 oranges in the basket how many apples are there ?

10) The ratio of boys to girls in a class is 2 : 5. If there are 12 boys how many girls are there ?

11) If there are 30 apples and 2 oranges in a fruit bowl, what is the missing ratio in its lowest term, apples : oranges = _ : 1

These are the subjects children liked at school. Use the data given to fill in the Venn diagram and answer the following:

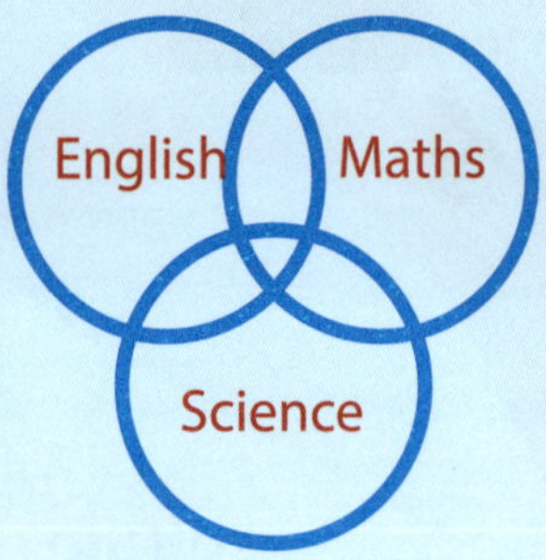

2 children liked Science
6 children liked English
9 children liked Maths
3 liked Maths and Science
7 liked English and Science
8 liked Maths and English
4 children liked all subjects

12) How many children liked English ?

13) How many children didn't like Maths ?

14) How many different subjects are there ?

15) How many children didn't like English ?

16) How many children liked Maths ?

17) How many children were in the group ?

22) What is the missing amount if 100 is divided in the ratio 7 : 3 = _ : 30 ?

DOWN

1) Simplify the ratio to its simplest form. Find the value of x. 81 : 9 = x : 1

3) Simplify the ratio to its simplest form. Find the value of x. 35 : 5 = x : 1

5) Simplify the ratio to its simplest form. Find the value of y. 45 : 18 = y : 2

The chart shows a student's mark in four exams. Write down the score for each one.

6) Science

7) History

8) Maths

9) English

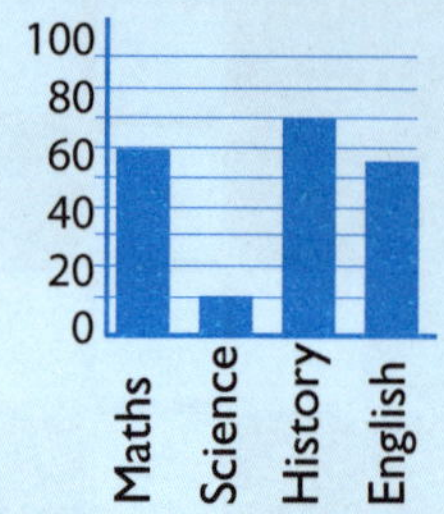

The Venn diagram shows what people were wearing.

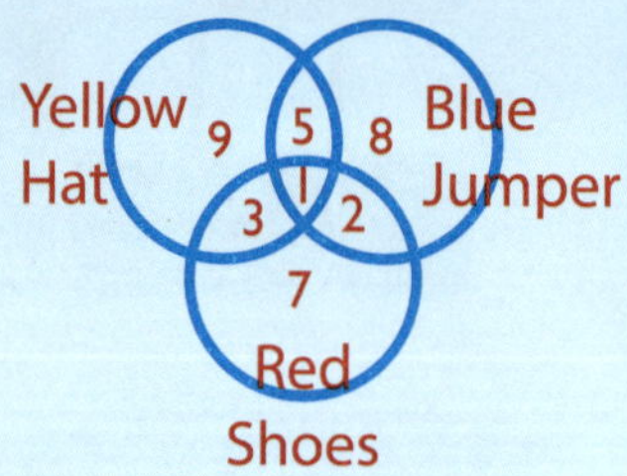

18) How many people were there altogether ?

19) How many people were not wearing a blue jumper ?

20) How many people were wearing a yellow hat ?

21) How many people were wearing a yellow hat and red shoes ?

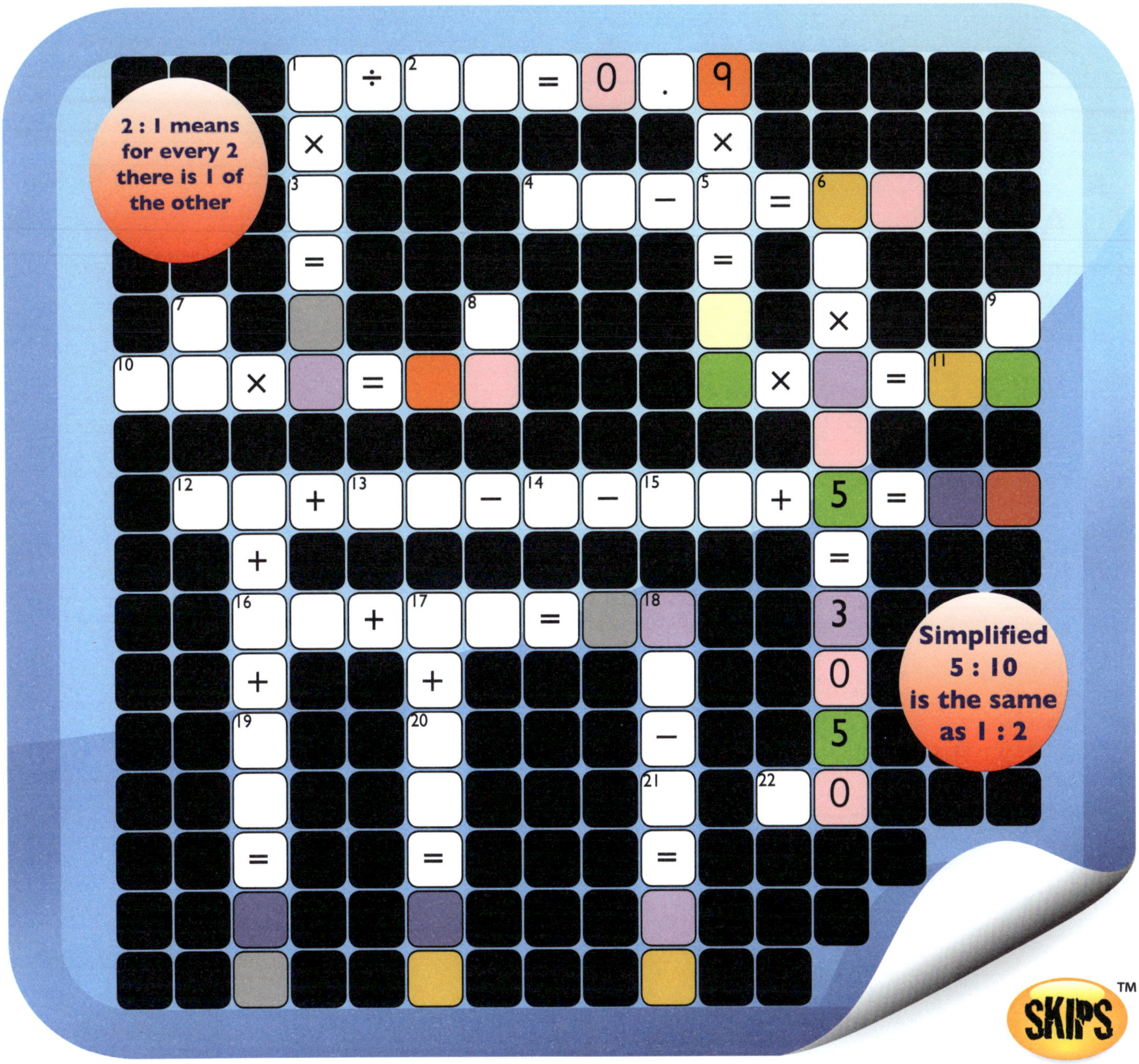

SKIPS CHALLENGE TIME!

Well Done! Now copy the numbers from the coloured tiles in the CrossMaths to the matching coloured boxes below and answer the following question.

Jack Pot saved £ ☐☐.

The ratio of *Jack's* saving to his friend *Robin Banks* is ☐ : ☐.

How much does *Robin* save ? £ __ __

CrossMaths 1

Use the clues below to complete the CrossMaths

ACROSS

1) How many faces does a cube have ?

3) Convert 45 mm into cm

5) Which one of these is an acute angle: 95°, 110°, 80°, 190°, 300° ?

7) What value does the digit 8 have in the number 4809 ?

10) Write $11\frac{3}{5}$ as a decimal

11) Round 5.17 to 1 decimal place

14) Convert 70% to a decimal

16) Write $\frac{17}{50}$ as a decimal

17) 6 → multiply by the product of three and 5 → ?

20) What is the area of the shape shown ?

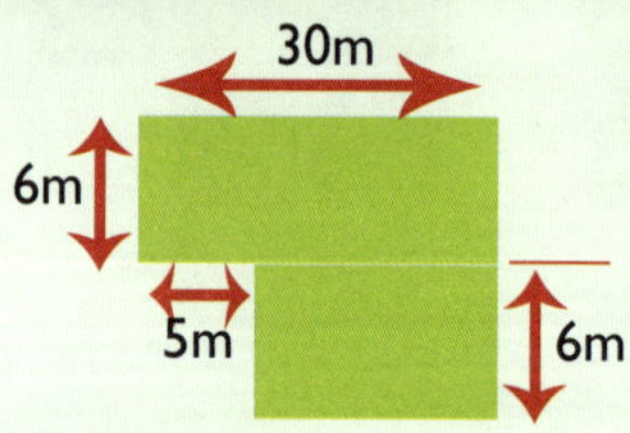

21) Write one thousand, three hundred and fifty

22) How many seconds are there in 19 minutes ?

DOWN

2) Which digit has a value of tenths in 123.45 ?

4) What is the square root of 81 ?

6) If 2x + 12 = 5x – 36, what is the value of x ?

8) How many sides does an octagon have ?

9) What is the sum of 25, 20 and 5 ?

12) What is the missing angle x ?

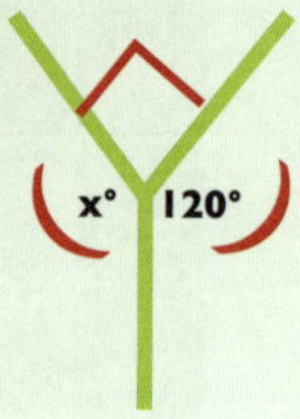

13) What is the reading x ?

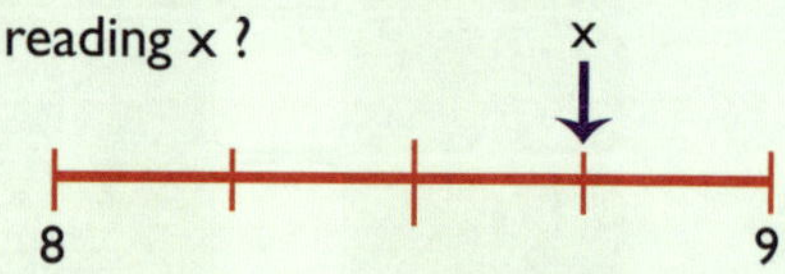

15) What is the area of the triangle ?

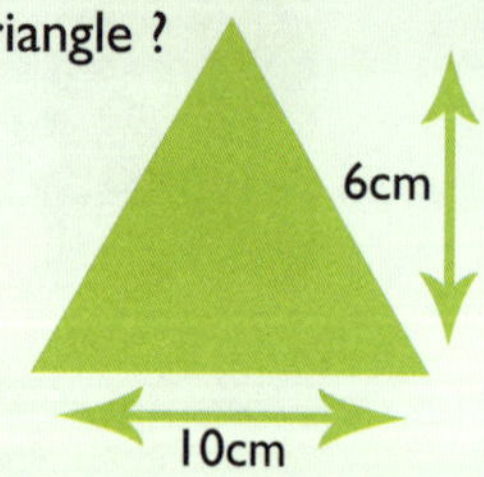

18) Reduce the value of 12 by 8

19) Mr Trot walks 1.4 km to work every day and at the end of the day walks back home again. How many kilometres does he walk over 5 days ?

Well Done SKIP!

SECTION 2

SKIPS Challenge Time! **Magic Numbers.**

Well Done! Now copy the numbers from the coloured tiles in the CrossMaths to the matching coloured boxes below and answer the following questions.

Dr. Hyno **can read your mind. He knows what number you are thinking about. Are you ready to test him? If so follow the steps below.**

He **wants you to think of any number and keep it in your head. Now *double* it.**

To the answer *add* [pink box] [blue box]. *Divide* your answer by [yellow box]. Finally *subtract* the first number you thought of.

Write your answer into this box [ ] ...and to prove *Dr. Hyno* knows your number take a look at page 55. *He asked the boy to write your number !!*

CrossMaths 2

Use the clues below to complete the CrossMaths

ACROSS

1) Write in figures nine thousand, four hundred and twenty one

2) Change the order of digits to make the largest number possible: 2 6 2 3

4) What is the missing angle x ?

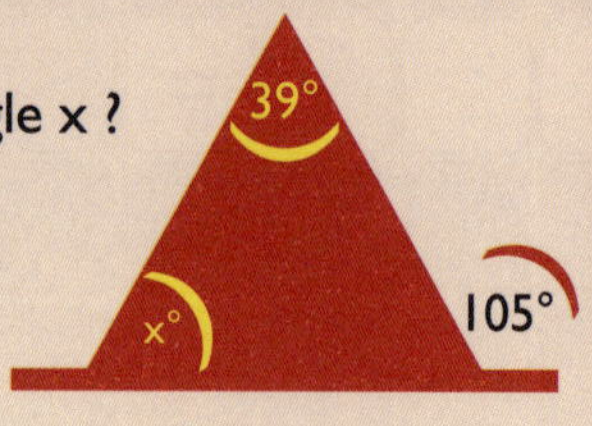

6) 12 is 3 more than half this number. What is the number ?

7) This number is 2 less than half of 20

10) What is the missing angle x ?

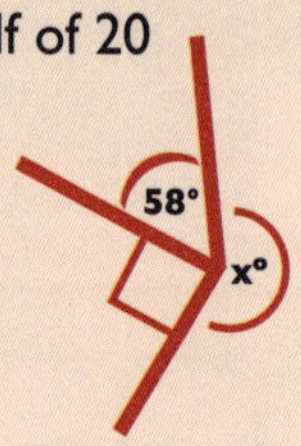

16) Calculate $\frac{5}{8}$ of 96

17) Convert 1.2 m into cm

19) If a boy stands facing north and turns 60 degrees to his right, how much in angles does he need to continue turning right to get back to facing north again ?

20) What value does the digit 9 have in 21936 ?

21) Look at the parallelogram and calculate angle x

22) A cube has a volume of $1000cm^3$. What is the area of each face ?

DOWN

3) What is the value of the digit 9 in the number 2397 ?

5) If $3x - 10 = 5$, what is x ?

8) What is the perimeter of the shape showm ?

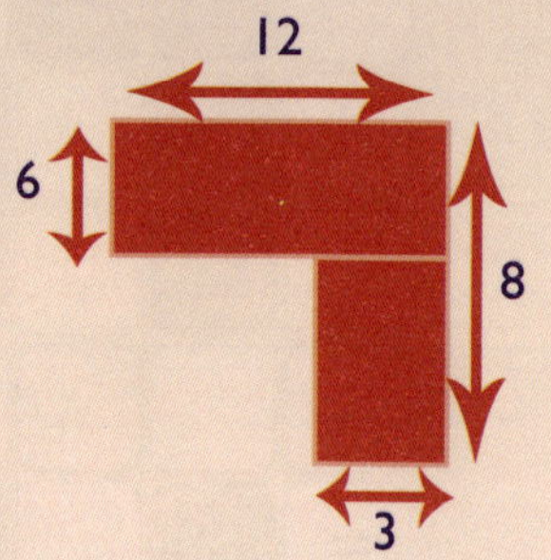

9) Write 75% as a fraction in its lowest term

11) Sarah set out from school at 3.30pm,. She goes to her gradma's and eventually gets home at 19.49. How many minutes after she left school did she arrive home ?

12) Write 0.05 as a fraction in its lowest term

13) Calculate $\frac{2}{5} \div 2$. Write your answer as a fraction.

14) Mr Tall measures his stride. It is 85 cm. If he takes 200 strides, how many metres has he gone ?

15) Mr Flick arrives at the cinemas at 18.30, the film starts at 19.25. How long, in minutes, must he wait until the film starts ?

18) If $3 (x + 4) = 5x - 10$, what is the value of x ?

SKIPS CHALLENGE TIME!

Well Done! Now copy the numbers from the coloured tiles in the CrossMaths to the matching coloured boxes below and answer the following question.

Tish Hughes **is now twice as old as her best friend,** ***Anita Hankey*****. In ☐ years time** ***Tish*** **will be ☐☐.**

How old will ***Anita*** **be then ? = __ __**

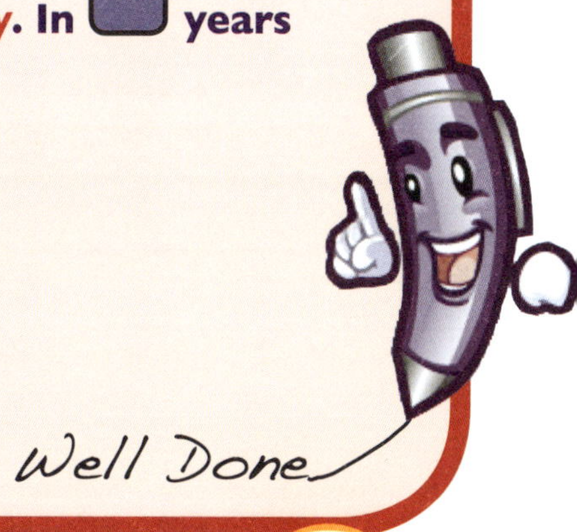

CrossMaths 3

Use the clues below to complete the CrossMaths

ACROSS

1) Which of these angles is an obtuse: 197°, 120°, 270°, 181°, 89° ?

2) What is the area of the shape shown ?

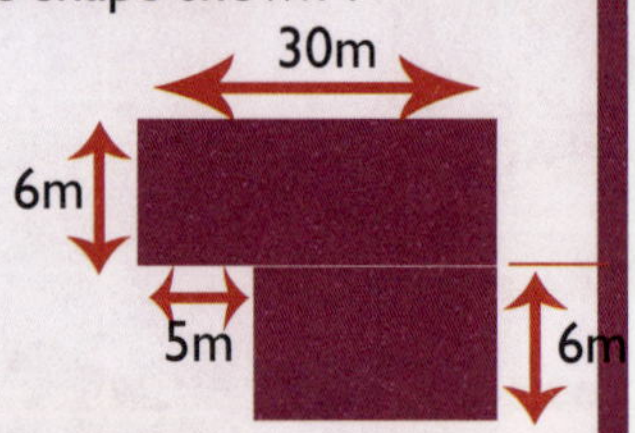

5) What value does the digit 8 have in 5486 ?

8) What is the sum of 34 mm, 56 mm and 26 mm (answer in cm) ?

10) In a theatre 25% of the seats were empty, but 306 seats were taken. How many empty seats were there ?

15) Divide 23 by 2

18) Calculate (8 – 4) x (20 ÷ 4)

19) If $x^2 + 6 = 150$, what is the value of x ?

20) Reduce forty by 21.

21) What is the missing angle ?

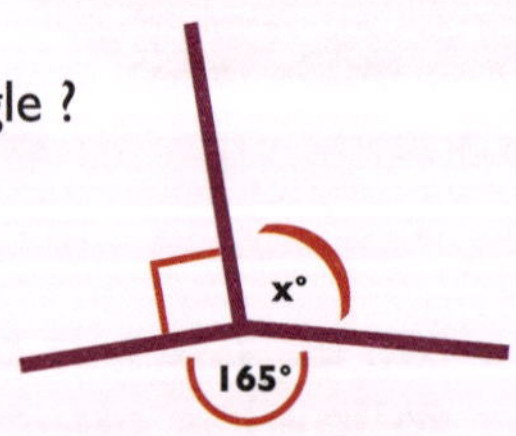

22) What is the difference between twelve dozen and fifty nine ?

23) Here is a sequence: 17, 15, 20, 18, 23, 21. What is the next number ?

DOWN

3) How many factors does the number 24 have ?

4) How many centimetres are there in 102 mm ?

6) Fifteen lots of three plus two lots of four equals ?

7) A triangle has an area of 18 cm^2 and a height of 4 cm. What is the base length ?

9) What is 18 out of 200 as a percentage ?

11) What is the missing angle ?

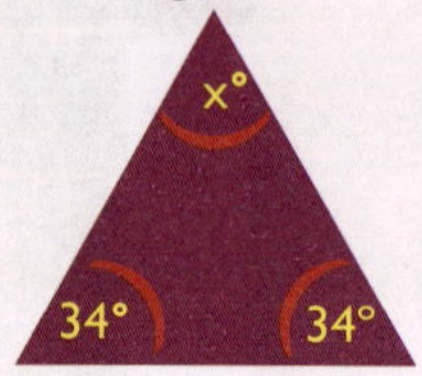

12) The machine multiplies by 5 and then adds 1. Which number has been put into the machine ?

? → FUNCTION → 102

13) Nicole's fat cat weighs 7950 grams. What is the cat's weight in kilograms ?

14) Write 50% as a fraction

16) What is the product of 2, 3, 5 ?

17) Which digit represents the value of hundredths in 1436.75 ?

24) If 12a – 20 = 4a + 4, what is the value of a ?

SKIPS CHALLENGE TIME!

Well Done! Now copy the numbers from the coloured tiles in the CrossMaths to the matching coloured boxes below and answer the following question.

Can you help *Pat Earn* find the next two numbers in the sequence?

A) ▢▢, ▢▢, ▢▢. __ __ __ __

B) ▢, ▢▢, ▢▢, ▢▢. __ __ __ __

C) ▢, ▢▢, ▢▢, ▢. __ __ __ __ __

CrossMaths 4

Use the clues below to complete the CrossMaths

ACROSS

1) Which number is exactly dividible by 7 and 21 from: 17, 27, 21, 41, 26 ?

2) What number lies half-way between 31 and 65 ?

3) Mr Fangs arrives early for his afternoon dentist appointment. He gets there at five to two, but his appointment is not until 14.04. How long does he have to wait ?

9) There are 35 pupils in a class. $\frac{4}{7}$ travel to school by bus, $\frac{2}{7}$ travel by car and the rest travel by skate board. How many pupils skate board to school ?

10) Convert 1100 m into km

14) What is the missing angle marked x ?

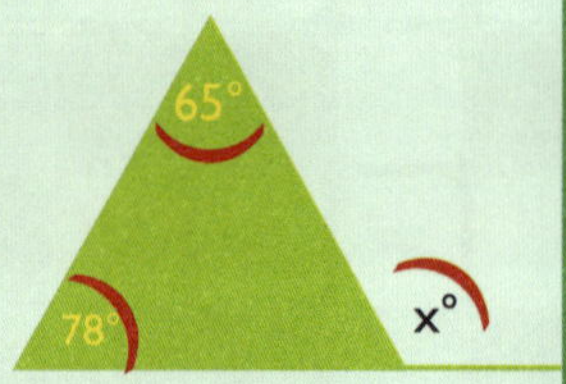

15) The area of a rectangle is 230 cm^2. It is 10 cm wide. What is its preimeter ?

17) A quadrilateral go-kart track has three angles 30°, 60°, and 100°. What is the size of the fourth angle ?

18) Divide 1416 by 6

19) This machine multiplies by 12 and then subtracts 2. Which number has been put into the machine ?

? → FUNCTION → 100

20) Convert 72 mm into cm

22) Divide 550 by 10^2

DOWN

4) Convert 0.91 km into m

5) Convert 0.498 kg into grams

6) What is the area of the triangle shown ?

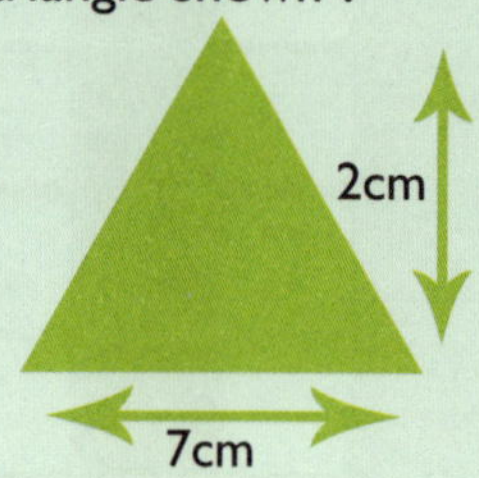

7) Round 7.7496 to two decimal places

8) A chocolate bar has 20 pieces. Mrs Chocky Chip eats 9 pieces. What percentage of the pieces is left ?

11) What is the missing angle marked x ?

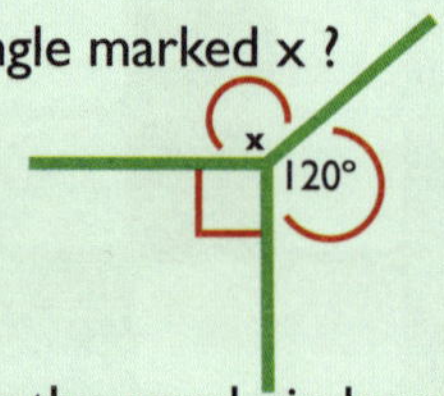

12) Write in figures twelve thousand, six hundred and fourty four

13) Subtract 43 from the product of 16 and 5

16) What is $2\frac{3}{5}$ as a decimal ?

17) What is the value of the digit 1 in 3145 ?

21) What is the next number in the sequence: 32, 42, 39, 49, 46 ?

Any four-sided shape is a quadrilateral

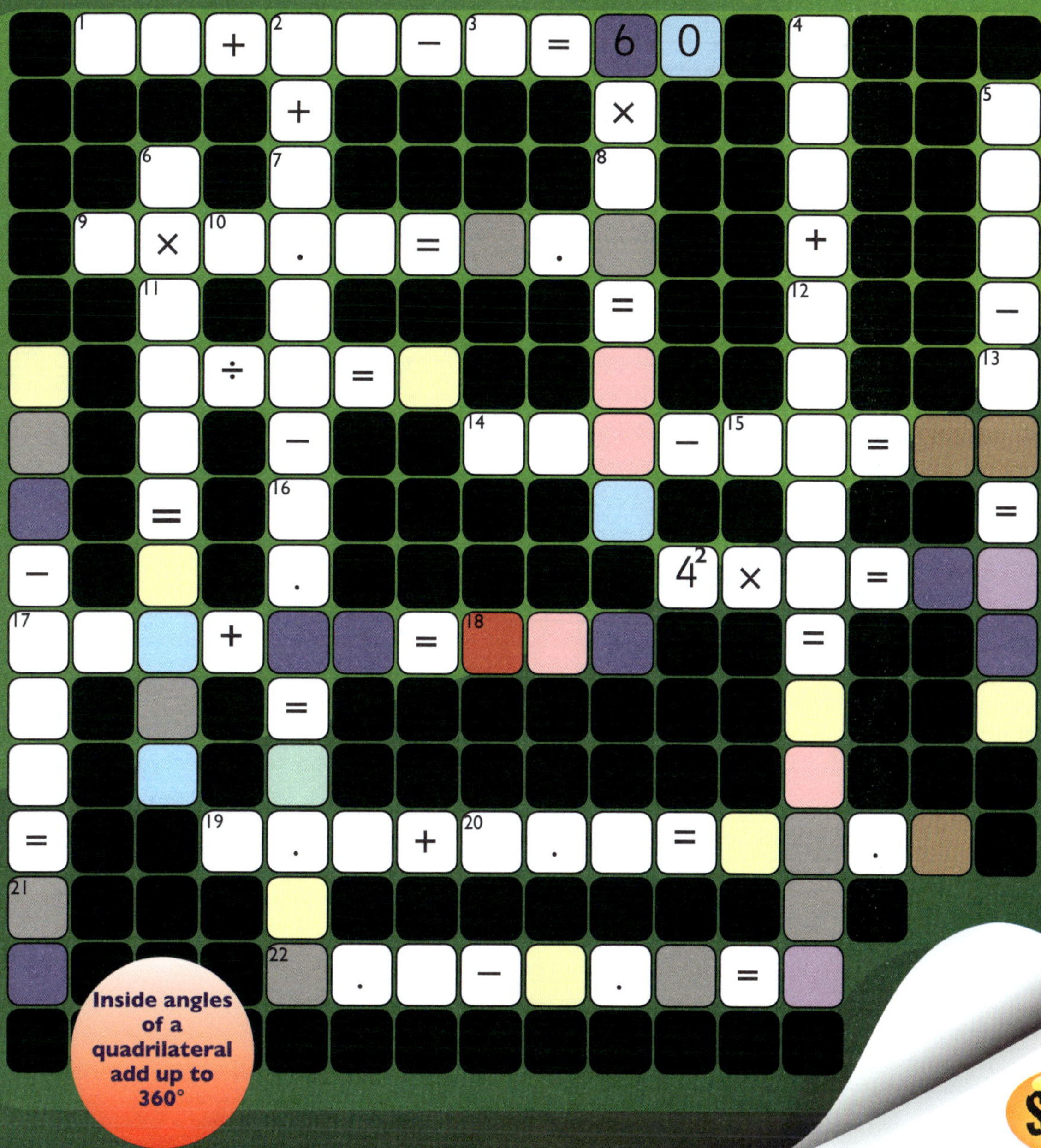

SKIPS CHALLENGE TIME!

Well Done! Now copy the numbers from the coloured tiles in the CrossMaths to the matching coloured boxes below and answer the following question.

Shiek Yiboudi **buys dancing shoes that cost £ [ ].[ ][ ] a pair.**

He then re-sells them at £ [ ].[ ][ ] a pair at the local market.

How much profit does he make if he sells [ ][ ][ ] pairs? **= £ ____**

CrossMaths 5

Use the clues below to complete the CrossMaths

ACROSS

1) What is 0.1146 when rounded to 2 decimal places ?

2) What is x ?

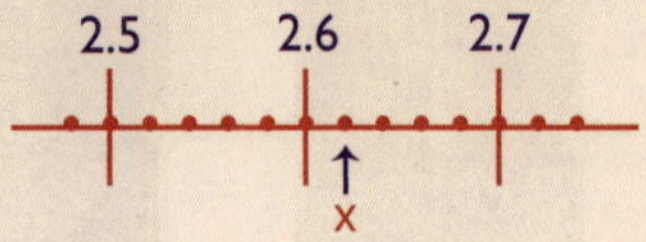

3) Write this improper fraction $\frac{56}{5}$ as a decimal

4) The pie chart shows how 44 children had their lessons at school today. How many did P.E ?

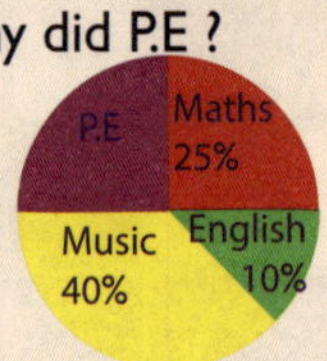

9) What is the perimeter of a rectangle which has measurements of length 19 cm and width 9 cm ?

12) If $20 - 2a = 4a + 2$, what is the value of a ?

13) A function machine multiplies by 5 and then adds 5. If 50 comes out what number goes into the machine ?

17) Which digit has a value of tenths in 36.24 ?

18) Which number lies half-way between 23 and 31 ?

20) Subtract three squared from the product of 3 and 5

21) Find the angle x

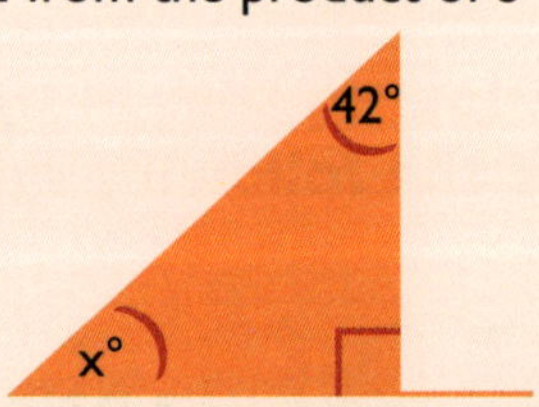

22) If $4x + 12 = 5x$, what is the value of x ?

23) What is the next number in the sequence: 47, 49, 53, 55, 59 ?

25) What is the median of this set of numbers: 25, 28, 31, 33, 19, 22, 23 ?

26) What is the value of y if $4y + 2 = 74$?

DOWN

5) What is 64.5 mm in cm ?

6) What is the volume of the cuboid shown ?

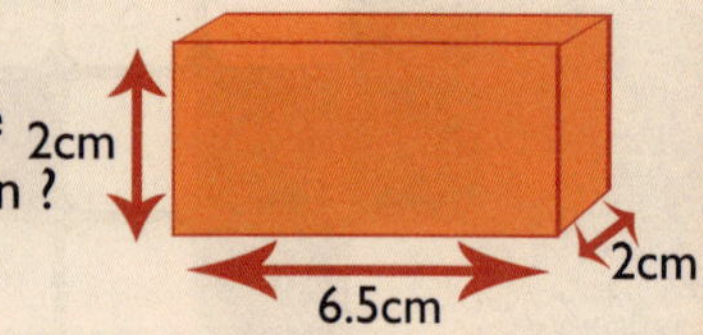

7) What is the missing angle x ?

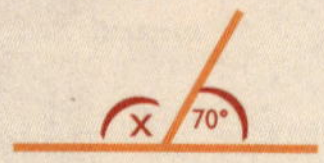

8) What is the area of the triangle ?

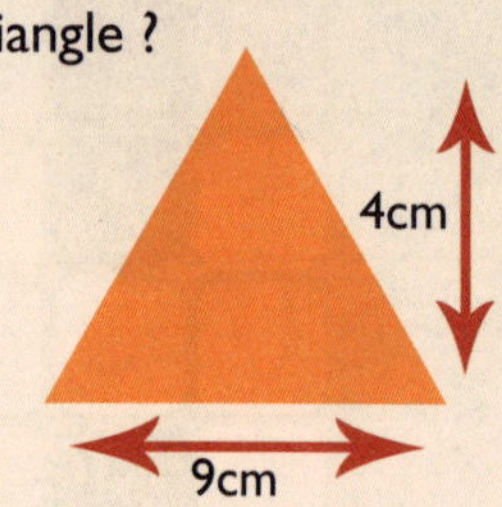

10) A spider drops to the bottom of a well 5 m deep. It crawled up 3 m each day but unfortunately slipped back 2 m every night. How many days does it take for the spider to climb to the top ?

11) What is the value of the 2 digit in the number 12401 ?

14) Which one of these is not a prime number: 5, 7, 9, 11, 17 ?

15) Calculate $3^3 - 2^2 - 2^3$

16) Lamb costs £3.50 per kilogram and fish costs £4.00 per kilogram. Mr Large buys 20 kg of lamb and 10 kg of fish. How much does he spend. (Write your answer in pounds) ?

19) Sacha is saving to buy Glenn Hoddle football boots costing £85. He saves £6.50 a week and already has £27 in savings. How many more weeks will he have to save before he has enough money to buy the boots ?

24) How many hours are there in 1440 minutes ?

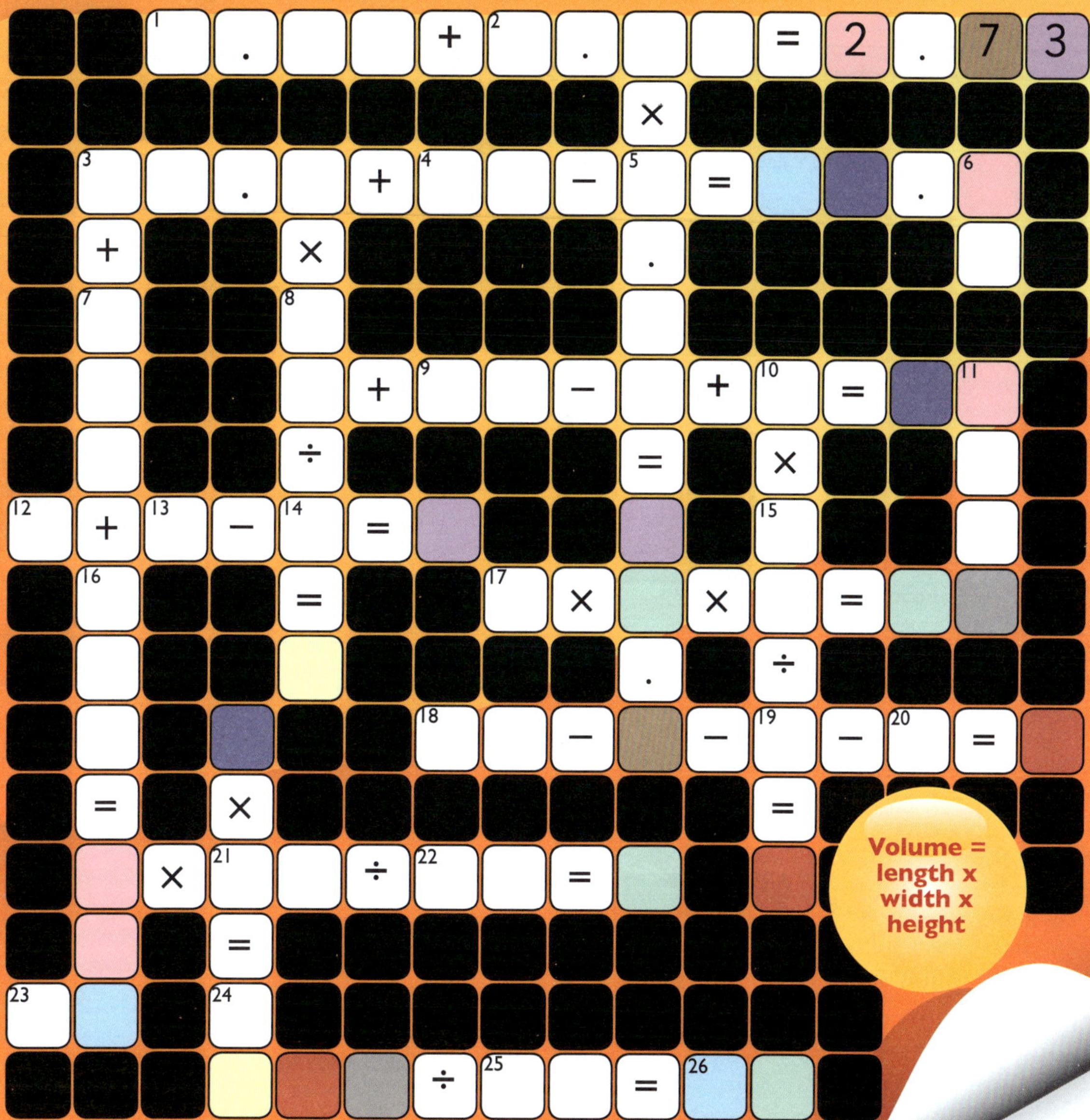

SKIPS™

SKIPS CHALLENGE TIME!

Well Done! Now copy the numbers from the coloured tiles in the CrossMaths to the matching coloured boxes below and complete the sentence.

Can you help *Ann Teak* to convert her analogue time to digital 24 hour time?

A) 1.45 a.m = ☐☐:☐☐

B) 12.00 p.m = ☐☐:☐☐

C) 11.15 p.m = ☐☐:☐☐

CrossMaths 6

Use the clues below to complete the CrossMaths

ACROSS

1) From the spinner, which number is more likely to come up ?

2) What is the area of the isosceles triangle shown ?

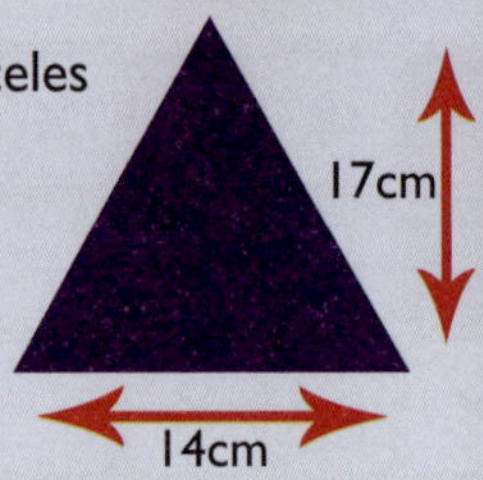

4) What is the area of a triangle that has a base length of 9 cm and a height of 4 cm ?

6) Round 3.56 to 1 decimal place

7) What is the perimeter of the shape shown ?

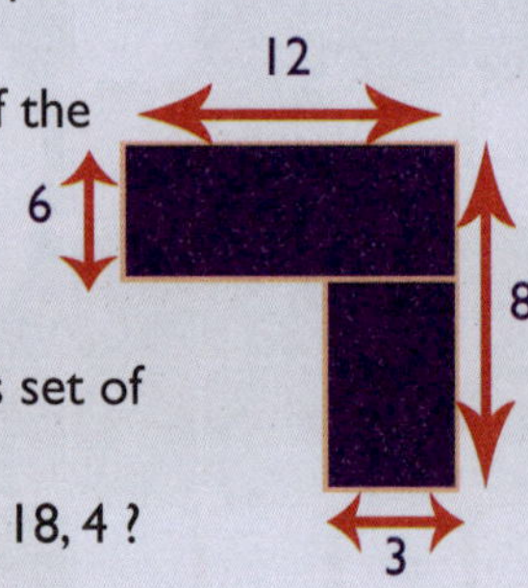

11) What is the mode of this set of numbers:
12, 14, 9, 14, 12, 12, 9, 15, 18, 4 ?

12) Hema gets three times more sweets than Shivam. If their dad gives them 16 sweets to share, how many sweets does Shivam get ?

13) If $3x + 22 = 5x - 4$, what is x ?

17) What do the angles inside a quadrilateral shape always add up to ?

18) Convert 90 mm into cm

The following bar line graph shows how high children can jump.

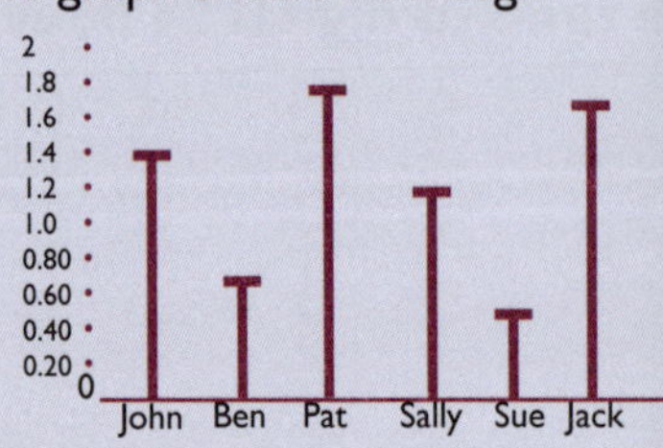

20) How high did Pat jump ?

21) How high did Sue jump ?

23) What value does the digit 2 represent in the number 12500 ?

DOWN

3) What is the missing number in the sequence:
14, 15, 21, ? 28, 29

5) From the diagram shown, what is the missing angle x ?

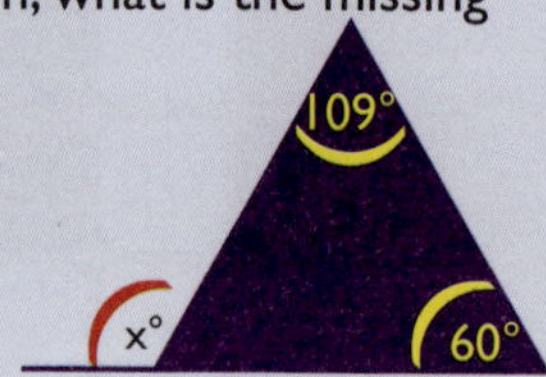

8) What is the height of the rectangle shown ?

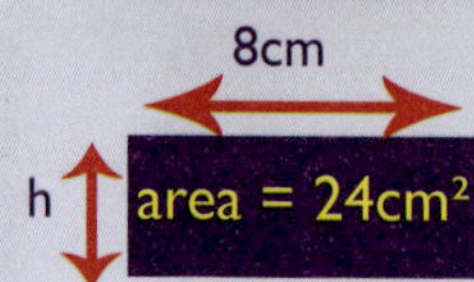

9) Two of the three angles of a triangle measure 35° and 44°, what is the size of the third angle ?

10) What is the median of these numbers:
25, 11, 12, 18, 26, 34, 21 ?

14) What number comes out of the function machine:

4 → SQUARE → ÷ 10 → ?

15) What is the value of the missing angle ?

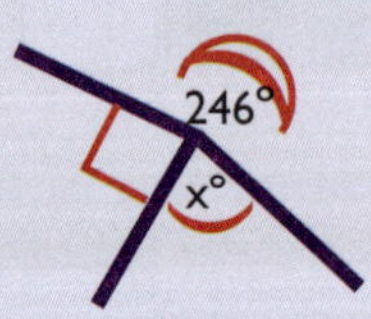

16) This function machine squares the number and then adds it to the product of 18 and 2. If number 3 goes into the machine, what number comes out ?

19) Write in figures one thousand, two hundred and three

22) $\frac{\square}{4} = \frac{30}{40}$

SKIPS CHALLENGE TIME!

Well Done! Now copy the numbers from the coloured tiles in the CrossMaths to the matching coloured boxes below and answer the following question.

***Di Rhea* has £ [pink][lilac]. She spends [pink]/[lilac] of it and then gives £ [blue].[green][yellow].**

to her friend *I. P. Daily*.

How much does *Di* have left? = £ __.__ __

CrossMaths 7

Use the clues below to complete the CrossMaths

ACROSS

1) What is the total area of the shape shown ?

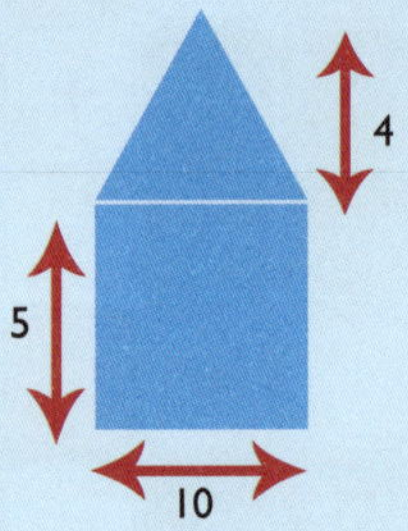

2) How many vertices does a cone have ?

3) Write $\frac{1}{10}$ as a decimal

8) There are 464 players at a football tournament. The teams are made up of 8 players each. How many teams are there altogether ?

14) Which one of these numbers is not a factor of 88:
4, 22, 2, 10, 8 ?

15) Which digit in the following number has a value of tenths: 23.54 ?

18) Calculate $(42 - 6) \div (2 \times 3)$

20) What is five percent of four hundred and eighty ?

21) Due to more people wanting to watch WBA play football, the length of the road outside had to be increased by 25%. The road was 800 metres long. How long is the road now in metres ?

22) What value does the digit 1 have in 5155.23 ?

23) Mr Large weighs 92 kg and decides to go on a diet. He loses 10% of his weight. What is his new weight ?

24) Convert the following: 718 mm = _ cm

DOWN

4) If the time is now 16:00. In how many more hours will it be midnight ?

5) Which one of these angles is a reflex angle:
45°, 112°, 230°, 175°, 90° ?

6) What is the mode of the following set of numbers:
91, 97, 94, 97, 92, 96, 97, 91 ?

7) What number comes out of the function machine ?
2 → Multiply by the sum of 10 and 8 → ?

9) What is the perimeter of a regular pentagon that has a side length of 88 cm ?

10) From the diagram shown what is the missing angle x ?

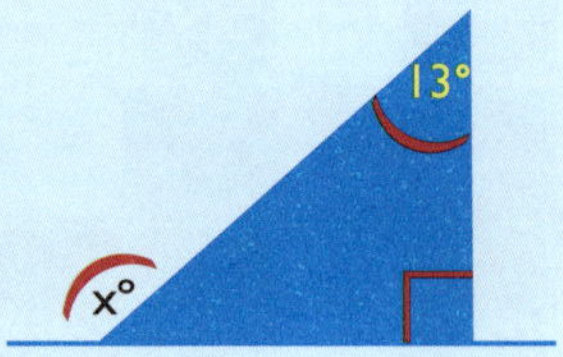

11) What is the missing angle on a trapezium that has 3 inside angles of: 122°, 65° and 85° ?

12) Write $\frac{6}{12}$ as a percentage

13) Halve the product of 4 and 29

16) Work out the value of y in the following equation:
$157 - y = 88$.

17) The girl to boy ratio is 3 : 4. If there are 30 girls, how many boys are there ?

19) Mrs Jude started a telephone conversation at 10.30 am. She talked until 13:50 . How many minutes was she on the telephone ?

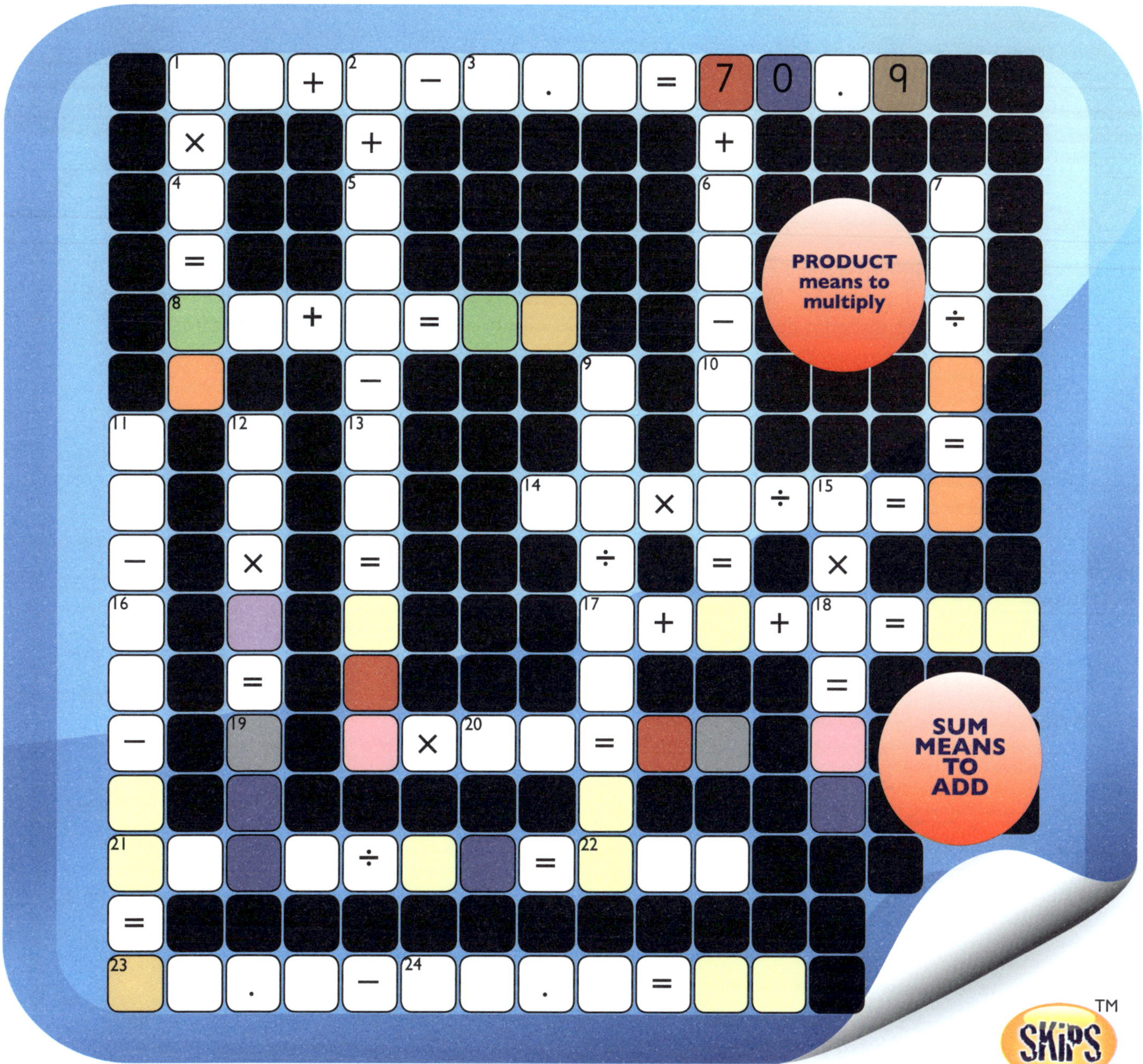

SKIPS™

SKIPS CHALLENGE TIME!

Well Done! **Now copy the numbers from the coloured tiles in the CrossMaths to the matching coloured boxes below and answer the following question.**

Ray Strack **travels for ▢▢ minutes, at a speed of ▢▢ km/h.**

He then stops for a break for ▢▢ minutes before continuing his journey

at ▢▢ km/h for ▢ hours.

What is the total distance travelled by *Ray* ? = _ _ _ km

CrossMaths 8

Use the clues below to complete the CrossMaths

ACROSS

1) Stan Still is buying some stationery for £43.20. Because he is spending over £30 he gets 10% reduction. How much discount does he get ?

2) Convert the following: 456 cm = _ m

5) A farmer plants 125 seeds in a tray. He puts the same number of seeds in each tray. If he uses 40 trays, how many seeds does he use altogether ?

7) You pay a 8% deposit when booking a holiday. If the total cost is £875. How much is the deposit ?

11) 178 people get onto a train. At the next stop 59 more people get on the train, whilst 67 people get off. How many people are now on the train?

12) What is the volume of the cuboid shown ?

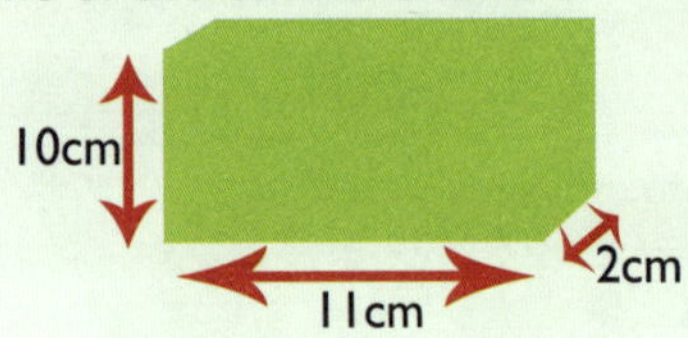

13) Convert the following: 0.231 km = _m

14) An adult train ticket costs £20.49 each and a child's ticket cost £18.59 each. What is the total cost if 3 adults and 3 children catch the train ?

16) What is the missing angle ?

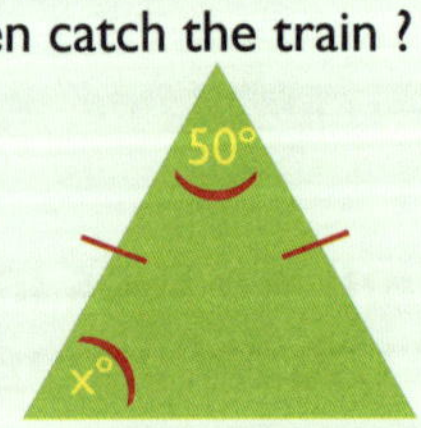

18) Sandra got 20 out of 80 in an English test. The teacher remarked the paper and this time she was awarded 75%. How many extra marks did the teacher give Sandra when she remarked the questions ?

19) Which digit has a value of hundredth's in 523.413 ?

20) Which digit has a value of hundreds in 2135.56 ?

DOWN

3) A bottle of water costs £1.15 and ice-creams cost 80p each. How much will it cost to buy 5 bottles of water and four ice-creams ? (Answer in pounds and pence)

4) What is the area of the shape shown ?

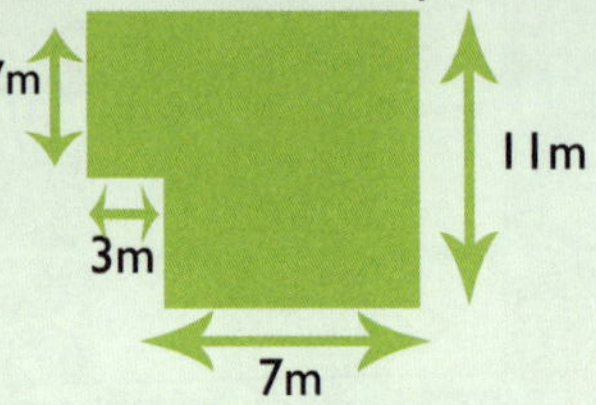

6) It costs £500 to hire a car for a week. A 5% deposit is paid when booking. How much is this deposit ?

8) The temperature inside the house is 40 degrees higher than it is outside. If the temperature outside is –7 degrees, what is the temperature inside ?

9) A picture costing £12.50 is reduced by 30% in a sale. What is the new price of the picture ? (Answer in pounds and pence)

10) Jumpers are boxed in fives. Mr Jones takes delivery of 43 boxes for his shop. How many jumpers have been delivered to his shop ?

15) An equalateral triangle has three equal sides and three equal angles. What is the size of the angles ?

17) Hexley uses his mobile phone to send text messages. Each text costs 5p and he sends 60 text messages a week. How much does he spend on text messages a week ? (Answer in pence)

SKIPS™

SKIPS CHALLENGE TIME!

Well Done! Now copy the numbers from the coloured tiles in the CrossMaths to the matching coloured boxes below and answer the following question.

Wayne Bow **has a rectangular money box which is [ ][ ] square centimetres.**

It is [ ][ ] centimetres tall. How wide is it ? [_] cm

CrossMaths 9

Use the clues below to complete the CrossMaths

ACROSS

1) A theatre can seat 400 people. Yesterday it was $\frac{11}{20}$ full. How many seats were full ?

2) Convert 0.625 litres into millilitres

3) What is 80% of 565 ?

5) Write this improper fraction as a decimal: $\frac{42}{20}$

7) What is the missing number in this sequence: 23, 24, 29, ?, 35, 36 ?

11) What is the mode of this set of numbers: 14, 17, 15, 15, 14, 17, 21, 17 ?

13) How many minutes are there in three hours and four minutes ?

14) What is the perimeter of a square which has a side length of 10 m ?

17) Round to two decimal places the number 55.494

18) Round this number to two decimal places 11.505

20) Which one of these is an acute angle: 95°, 110°, 80°, 190°, 300° ?

21) Complete the following function machine

15 → [−12] → [x 3] → ?

22) What is the missing angle x on this isosceles triangle ?

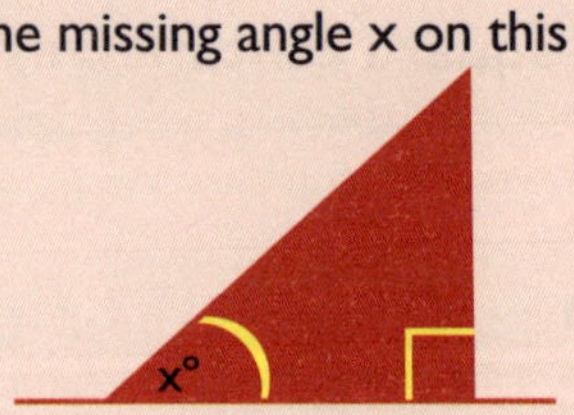

23) What is the value of seven squared ?

DOWN

4) What value does the digit 7 have in the number 3271 ?

6) Calculate $\frac{2}{5} - \frac{6}{20}$ (Answer in lowest term)

8) If the area of a triangle is 12 cm^2 and its base length is 8 cm, what is its height ?

9) Calculate $(5 \times 9) - (6^2 + 3)$

10) Work out $1\frac{1}{2} \div 1\frac{2}{3}$

12) What is x if 4x + 2 = 74 ?

15) What is the missing number in the following sequence:
5 ? 11 15 17 21

16) Convert 460 mm into cm

19) What is the median of this set of numbers: 13, 11, 16, 9, 10, 18 ?

24) A function machine squares the number then adds it to the product of 4 and 9. If the number 3 goes into the machine what number comes out ?

SKIPS CHALLENGE TIME!

Well Done! Now copy the numbers from the coloured tiles in the CrossMaths to the matching coloured boxes below and answer the following question.

Price Wright **spends £ ☐☐.☐☐ on ☐ coats. The coats both cost the same amount.**

What is the cost of each coat = ? £__ __.__ __

CrossMaths 10

Use the clues below to complete the CrossMaths

ACROSS

2) Sacha is now twice his sisters age. In four years time Sacha will be 16. How old will his sister be then ?

3) Calculate $5^3 \times 2^2 \div 5$

4) What is the volume of a cuboid that is 25 cm long 3 cm tall and 4 cm wide ?

9) What is the sum of 9 squared plus 9 ?

10) Calculate 11 out of 20 as a percentage

11) If $x^2 + 11 = 20$, what is the value of x ?

14) 33 children are going on a trip to Italy. The trip costs £25 each. How much money should be collected in total from all the children ?

16) Double the difference between 125 and 476

17) A machine divides by five and then multiplies by three. If 185 goes into the machine what number comes out ?

21) Which digit has a value of hundredths in 769.48 ?

22) How many equal angles does an isosceles triangle have ?

24) $3a + 7b - 4c = x$. If a = 6, b = 5 and c = 8, what is the value of x ?

25) In the parallelogram angle y measures 110°. What is the size of angle x ?

DOWN

1) Round 31.72 to the nearest whole number

5) Write 6.5284 to two decimal places

6) A box holds 6 cups. How many boxes will be needed to hold 102 cups ?

7) How many vertices does a triangular based pyramid have ?

8) The perimeter of a rectangle is 18 cm. If the longest side is 6 cm, what is the area ?

12) Helen is going on holiday which cost £180. Each week she pays £15 towards the cost. So far she has paid £75. How many more weekly payments does she need to make ?

13) If $5a + 9 = 6a - 3$, what is the value a ?

15) Nicole's mum buys her a new longer skirt in a sale at half price. The original cost of the skirt was £9.50. How much change did Nicole's mum get from a £10 note ?
(Answer in pounds and pence)

18) A rectangle has an area of 54 cm^2. If two of the sides are both 6cm long, what is the length of each of the other two sides ?

19) 525 raffle tickets were sold by 25 pupils in one school. On average how many tickets did each pupil sell ?

20) The WBA football magazine has 56 pages. $\frac{2}{7}$ of the pages contain typing errors.
How many pages contain typing errors ?

23) What is the volume of a box which has measurements of length 7 cm, height 4 cm and width 2 cm ?

26) Calculate $\frac{2}{5} + \frac{9}{10} - \frac{6}{20}$

SKIPS CHALLENGE TIME!

Well Done! Now copy the numbers from the coloured tiles in the CrossMaths to the matching coloured boxes below and answer the following question.

Walter Melon **bought a bunch of bananas for £ __.__ __ and __ bunches of grapes that cost £ __.__ __ each.**

How much change should he receive from £ __ __.__ __ ?

Answer = £ __.__ __

SECTION 3

ANSWERS:

Well Done. Now check your answers and see how many questions you answered correctly.

Good Luck!

Page 2 NUMBERS

ACROSS		DOWN	
1	**2**	7	**5**
2	**33**	10	**8**
3	**78**	11	**5**
4	**70**	12	**88**
5	**50**	14	**10**
6	**35**	15	**6**
8	**25**	16	**3**
9	**16**	17	**11**
13	**75**	20	**8**
18	**25**	21	**30**
19	**28**	23	**21**
22	**22**		

0, 1, 2, 3, 4, 5, 6, 7, 8, 9

SKIPS Challenge
A) 6, 7, 7, 9
B) 2,1,1

Page 4 PLACE VALUE

ACROSS		DOWN	
2	**1.1**	1	**40**
4	**9.6**	3	**5**
5	**4.6**	6	**2**
9	**6**	7	**30**
11	**7**	8	**4.65**
13	**11**	10	**2.5**
14	**5**	12	**5**
19	**80**	15	**55**
20	**50**	16	**2.5**
22	**5.5**	17	**1.8**
		18	**7**
		21	**2**

2, 0, 6, 1, 3, 5

SKIPS Challenge
A) 3, 5, 0, 6
Answer: £6530
B) 6, 2, 1, 5
Answer: £1256

Page 6 FACTORS AND MULTIPLES

ACROSS		DOWN	
3	**3**	1	**12**
4	**4**	2	**20**
7	**2**	5	**30**
8	**2**	6	**8**
15	**24**	9	**4**
16	**3**	10	**44**
17	**5**	11	**23**
19	**78**	12	**6**
20	**42**	13	**8**
21	**4**	14	**48**
		18	**2**

6, 8, 2, 3, 1, 4, 0, 7, 5

SKIPS Challenge
£2.50, £30,
Answer: 12

Page 8 FRACTIONS

ACROSS		DOWN	
2	$\frac{5}{11}$	1	$\frac{1}{2}$
4	$\frac{3}{4}$	3	$\frac{4}{11}$
5	$\frac{1}{2}$	7	$\frac{1}{5}$
6	$\frac{4}{11}$	10	8
8	$\frac{6}{11}$	11	$\frac{2}{3}$
9	4	14	$\frac{5}{2}$
12	$\frac{1}{3}$	15	$\frac{4}{5}$
13	$\frac{1}{2}$	16	$\frac{1}{3}$
18	$\frac{1}{4}$	17	3
21	$\frac{1}{2}$	19	5
		20	4
		22	$\frac{3}{2}$

4, 2, 8, 0, 9, 1, 5, $\frac{1}{4}$, $\frac{1}{5}$, $\frac{5}{11}$, $\frac{9}{11}$

SKIPS Challenge
A) $\frac{18}{22}$ **Answer:** $\frac{9}{11}$
B) $\frac{10}{40}$ **Answer:** $\frac{1}{4}$

Page 10 DECIMALS

ACROSS		DOWN	
2	**5**	1	**4**
3	**10**	4	**0.2**
7	**30**	5	**1010**
9	**5**	6	**20**
10	**0.5**	8	**1.42**
14	**10.78**	11	**6.12**
17	**4.33**	12	**100**
18	**16.7**	13	**997**
19	**4.2**	15	**16**
20	**9.2**	16	**5**

6, 8, 2, 4, 0, 3, 5, 1, 9

SKIPS Challenge
6840, 5132
Answer: 1708

Page 14 Fractions,Decimals, Percentages

ACROSS		DOWN	
1	$\frac{3}{10}$	5	$\frac{7}{10}$
2	**0.7**	7	**8**
3	**9**	8	**4**
4	**4**	9	**0.6**
6	**12**	10	**4.2**
12	**45**	11	**20**
14	**2.1**	13	**2**
15	**1.2**	16	**8**
19	**78**	17	**0.1**
20	**0.18**	18	**8**

7 0 5 2 4 3 8 9 1 6

SKIPS Challenge

75, 60

Answer: 15

Page 16 PERIMETERS, AREAS, COMPOUND SHAPES

ACROSS		DOWN	
2	**4**	1	**4**
3	**40**	4	**8**
6	**32**	5	**24**
7	**28**	11	**28**
8	**6**	12	**44**
9	**9**	13	**16**
10	**30**	14	**32**
17	**80**	15	**48**
18	**12**	16	**32**
19	**92**	20	**10**

8 6 4 0 2 1 5 3 9

SKIPS Challenge

A) 10,25 Answer: 125

B) 32, 12 Answer: 1) 4

2) 48

Page 18 ANGLES

ACROSS		DOWN	
1	**80**	3	**75**
2	**60**	4	**45**
8	**12**	5	**80**
9	**3**	6	**69**
10	**6**	7	**230**
11	**3**	12	**160**
12	**180**	13	**125**
16	**55**	14	**175**
18	**95**	15	**77**
19	**25**	17	**25**

5 4 7 2 9 1 6 8 3 0

SKIPS Challenge

90, 90, 90, 180, 180

Page 20 MEASUREMENTS

ACROSS		DOWN	
1	**40**	9	**970**
2	**2**	4	**600**
6	**6000**	5	**20**
10	**50**	7	**103**
12	**7**	8	**320**
13	**16**	9	**70**
14	**6392**	11	**21**
16	**5**	15	**4**
19	**600**	17	**9**
20	**303**	18	**72**

4 5 6 0 9 1 2 8 3 7

SKIPS Challenge

1.6, $\frac{3}{4}$ **Answer: 400**

Page 22 BRACKETS

ACROSS		DOWN	
1	**24**	4	**725**
2	**16**	6	**50**
3	**63**	9	**0.25**
5	**115**	10	**5**
7	**75**	11	**1.15**
8	**60**	13	**25**
12	**1**	14	**70**
16	**500**	15	**18**
17	**50**	18	**0.5**
21	**8**	19	**75**
24	**150**	20	**330**
		22	**4**
		23	**4**

6, 5, 8, 0, 2, 4, 1, 9, 3, 7

SKIPS Challenge
5, 2, 5, £2.25, £1.20
Answer: £1.50

Page 24 ALGEBRA

ACROSS		DOWN	
1	**3**	3	**5**
2	**4**	4	**4**
8	**40**	5	**8**
9	**10**	6	**24**
11	**36**	7	**4**
16	**7**	10	**10**
17	**19**	12	**12**
18	**5**	13	**27**
19	**5**	14	**8**
20	**125**	15	**30**

8, 5, 9, 4, 6, 2, 1, 7, 3, 0

SKIPS Challenge
A) 8, 4, 6 Answer: 18
B) 7, 3, 9 Answer: 34

Page 26 AVERAGES

ACROSS		DOWN	
1	**6**	3	**100**
2	**9**	4	**4**
7	**5**	5	**10**
13	**12**	6	**8**
14	**44**	8	**8**
15	**44**	9	**10**
16	**180**	10	**42**
17	**8**	11	**38**
19	**142**	12	**48**
20	**30**	18	**54**

0, 1, 2, 3, 4, 5, 6, 8, 9

SKIPS Challenge
60, 45, 26, 14, 14, 21
Answer: A) 14 B) 30 C) 46

Page 28 RATIOS, HANDLING DATA

ACROSS		DOWN	
2	**10**	1	**9**
4	**15**	3	**7**
10	**30**	5	**5**
11	**15**	6	**10**
12	**25**	7	**70**
13	**15**	8	**60**
14	**3**	9	**55**
15	**14**	18	**35**
16	**24**	19	**19**
17	**39**	20	**18**
22	**70**	21	**4**

5, 6, 9, 4, 0, 8, 1, 3, 2

SKIPS Challenge
£40, 8, 5
Answer: £25

Page 30 CrossMaths 1

ACROSS		DOWN	
1	**6**	2	**4**
3	**4.5**	4	**9**
5	**80**	6	**16**
7	**800**	8	**8**
10	**11.6**	9	**50**
11	**5.2**	12	**150**
14	**0.7**	13	**8.75**
16	**0.34**	15	**30**
17	**90**	18	**4**
20	**330**	19	**14**
21	**1350**		
22	**1140**		

0 6 9 2 1 4 8 3 5

SKIPS Challenge
14, 2
Answer: 7

Page 32 CrossMaths 2

ACROSS		DOWN	
1	**9421**	3	**90**
2	**6322**	5	**5**
4	**66**	8	**40**
6	**18**	9	$\frac{3}{4}$
7	**8**		
10	**212**	11	**259**
16	**60**	12	$\frac{1}{20}$
17	**120**		
19	**300**	13	$\frac{1}{5}$
20	**900**		
21	**110**	14	**170**
22	**100**	15	**55**
		18	**11**

5 8 1 2 0 9 6 3 4

SKIPS Challenge
4,16
Answer: 10

Page 34 CrossMaths 3

ACROSS		DOWN	
1	**120**	3	**8**
2	**330**	4	**10.2**
5	**80**	6	**53**
8	**11.6**	7	**9**
10	**102**	9	**9**
15	**11.5**	11	**112**
18	**20**	12	**20.2**
19	**12**	13	**7.95**
20	**19**	14	$\frac{1}{2}$
21	**105**		
22	**85**	16	**30**
23	**26**	17	**5**
		24	**3**

3 6 0 8 1 4 9 2 5

SKIPS Challenge
A) 3, 8, 13, 18 Answer: 23, 28
B) 9, 16, 23, 30 Answer: 37, 44
C) 4, 8, 16, 32 Answer: 64, 128

Page 36 CrossMaths 4

ACROSS		DOWN	
1	**21**	4	**910**
2	**48**	5	**498**
3	**9**	6	**7**
9	**5**	7	**7.75**
10	**1.1**	8	**55**
14	**143**	11	**150**
15	**66**	12	**12644**
17	**170**	13	**37**
18	**236**	16	**2.6**
19	**8.5**	17	**100**
20	**7.2**	21	**56**
22	**5.5**		

5 2 1 7 3 0 9 4 6

SKIPS Challenge
£4.50, £6.50, 300
Answer: £600

Page 38 CrossMaths 5

ACROSS		DOWN	
1	**0.11**	5	**6.45**
2	**2.62**	6	**26**
3	**11.2**	7	**110**
4	**11**	8	**18**
9	**56**	10	**3**
12	**3**	11	**2000**
13	**9**	14	**9**
17	**2**	15	**15**
18	**27**	16	**110**
20	**6**	19	**9**
21	**48**	24	**24**
22	**12**		
23	**61**		
25	**25**		
26	**18**		

0 5 4 7 2 1 8 3 6

SKIPS Challenge
A) 01:45
B) 12:00
C) 23:15

Page 40 CrossMaths 6

ACROSS		DOWN	
1	**2**	3	**22**
2	**119**	5	**169**
4	**18**	8	**3**
6	**3.6**	9	**101**
7	**40**	10	**21**
11	**12**	14	**1.6**
12	**4**	15	**24**
13	**13**	16	**45**
17	**360**	19	**1203**
18	**9**	22	**3**
20	**1.8**		
21	**0.5**		
23	**2000**		

9 7 8 0 4 1 3 5 2 6

SKIPS Challenge
12, $\frac{1}{2}$, £3.50

Answer: £2.50

Page 42 CrossMaths 7

ACROSS		DOWN	
1	**70**	4	**8**
2	**1**	5	**230**
3	**0.1**	6	**97**
8	**58**	7	**36**
14	**10**	9	**440**
15	**5**	10	**103**
18	**6**	11	**88**
20	**24**	12	**50**
21	**1000**	13	**58**
22	**100**	16	**69**
23	**82.8**	17	**40**
24	**71.8**	19	**200**

5, 2, 6, 1, 8, 3, 9, 7, 4, 0

SKIPS Challenge
30, 60, 30, 50, 2
Answer: 130

Page 44 CrossMaths 8

ACROSS		DOWN	
1	**4.32**	3	**8.95**
2	**4.56**	4	**98**
5	**5000**	6	**25**
7	**70**	8	**33**
11	**170**	9	**8.75**
12	**220**	10	**215**
13	**231**	15	**60**
14	**117.24**	17	**300**
16	**65**		
18	**40**		
19	**1**		
20	**1**		

8, 1, 9, 0, 3, 2, 7, 5, 4

SKIPS Challenge
90, 15
Answer: 6

Page 46 CrossMaths 9

ACROSS		DOWN	
1	**220**	4	**70**
2	**625**	6	$\frac{1}{10}$
3	**452**		
5	**2.1**	8	**3**
7	**30**	9	**6**
11	**17**	10	$\frac{9}{10}$
13	**184**		
14	**40**	12	**18**
17	**55.49**	15	**9**
18	**11.51**	16	**46**
20	**80**	19	**12**
21	**9**	24	**45**
22	**45**		
23	**49**		

0, 1, 2, 3, 4, 5, 6, 7, 9

SKIPS Challenge
£70.24, 2
Answer: £35.12

Page 48 CrossMaths 10

ACROSS		DOWN	
2	**10**	1	**32**
3	**100**	5	**6.53**
4	**300**	6	**17**
9	**90**	7	**4**
10	**55**	8	**18**
11	**3**	12	**7**
14	**825**	13	**12**
16	**702**	15	**5.25**
17	**111**	18	**9**
21	**8**	19	**21**
22	**2**	20	**16**
24	**21**	23	**56**
25	**70**	26	**1**

0, 1, 2, 3, 4, 5, 6, 8, 9

SKIPS Challenge
£5.65, 4, £1.35, £20.00
Answer: £8.95

NOTES:

NOTES:

ORDER FORM

	TITLE		RRP
	**SKIPS KS1 CrossWord Puzzles** Key Stage 1 English	ISBN 978-0-9567526-5-9	£7.99
	**SKIPS KS1 CrossMaths Puzzles** Key Stage 1 Maths	ISBN 978-0-9567526-4-2	£7.99
	**SKIPS KS2 CrossWord Puzzles** Key Stage 2 English Book 1	ISBN 978-0-9567526-6-6	£7.99
	**SKIPS KS2 CrossWord Puzzles** Key Stage 2 English Book 2	ISBN 978-0-9567526-2-8	£7.99
	**SKIPS KS2 CrossMaths Puzzles** Key Stage 2 Maths Book 1	ISBN 978-0-9567526-7-3	£7.99
	**SKIPS KS2 CrossMaths Puzzles** Key Stage 2 Maths Book 2	ISBN 978-0-9567526-3-5	£7.99
	**SKIPS 11+ CrossWord Puzzles** 11 Plus English	ISBN 978-0-9567526-0-4	£9.99
	**SKIPS 11+ CrossMaths Puzzles** 11 Plus Maths	ISBN 978-0-9567526-1-1	£9.99

Teachers and Tutors

You will be eligible for discounts on purchases of sets of 10 copies or more. Please get in touch for more details.

sales@skipscrosswords.co.uk

www.skipscrosswords.co.uk

SKIPS Crosswords
142 Newton Road, Great Barr
Birmingham B43 6BT
United Kingdom

For more SKIPS titles visit our website.